Applied Econometrics:

A Simple Introduction

Also by K.H. Erickson

Simple Introductions

Accounting and Finance Formulas
Applied Econometrics
Choice Theory
Corporate Finance Formulas
eBay
Econometrics
Economics
Financial Economics
Financial Risk Management
Game Theory
Game Theory for Business
International Relations
Investment Appraisal
Investment Formulas
Marketing Management Concepts and Tools
Mathematical Formulas for Economics and Business
Methods of Microeconomics
Microeconomics

Applied Econometrics:

A Simple Introduction

K.H. Erickson

Contents

1 Introduction

This book applies established econometric concepts and methods to a large sample of empirical financial market data, to provide both an insight into the potential real world applications of econometrics, and a detailed examination of the financial investment market over the chosen period. Building on basic econometrics knowledge and theory the book explores the issues which economic and financial data can present in practice. There is extensive use of graphs and model values throughout the book, all calculated with OxMetrics econometric software.

The next section explains the selection of the equities, commodities and risk-free rate of return data which comprise the datasets for this book, and notes how this data will be used to conduct analysis. Three chapters then follow which look at price, return and volatility analysis in turn. Price analysis first examines the distribution of data, then tests for stationarity, using Autocorrelation Functions (ACF) and Partial Autocorrelation Functions (PACF), and a Dickey-Fuller (DF) unit root test. Next data is differenced to ensure stationarity is met, followed by cointegration tests, with the Engle-Granger 2 step method and Error Correction Model (ECM), and the Johansen technique and Vector Error Correction Model (VECM).

Returns are what ultimately motivate financial market investors, and changes in prices are used to give returns for a chapter on return analysis. Return data is examined for Autoregressive (AR) and Moving Average (MA) processes, and the two are combined to form an ARMA model with the Box-Jenkins method. The Akaike Information Criterion (AIC) is then used to calculate the ARMA model which best fits the data, and to find the number of AR and MA lags required to accurately model the equities, commodities, and risk-free rate returns data.

Risk is the other area which concerns investors, and a chapter explores this in depth. With an ARMA model used to model returns a Generalized Autoregressive Conditionally Heteroskedastic (GARCH) model can be used to model the return conditional variance. The Akaike Information Criterion (AIC) is again used to find the optimum number of lags for this GARCH variance model, for each of the equities, commodities, and risk-free rate datasets. After the number of lags is decided GARCH model variations are assessed to improve the accuracy of the conditional variance model further, and the AIC compares EGARCH, GJR-GARCH, and GARCH-M variations. The chosen variation is then used to find the GARCH model variance, and from there the model volatility and risk.

With optimal ARMA and GARCH models selected, and return and volatility mean values calculated for the equities, commodities, and risk-free rate data, the issue of a portfolio management strategy can then be examined. First, a dynamic portfolio management strategy is analysed, using the Sharpe Ratio portfolio performance evaluation tool. The popular strategy to sell off equities and replace them with commodities during market downturns is explored in the midst of the 2007-2008 global financial crisis, as the performance of portfolios which stuck by equities are compared to those which switched to commodities.

A static unchanging portfolio management strategy is examined, using the optimal ARMA and GARCH models calculated earlier, and using the empirical relationship between equities and commodities to determine the portfolio weighting for the different assets. The model's forecasted returns, volatility and variance are then compared to the actual empirical returns and volatility, to determine the accuracy of forecasts and assess the strategy of holding an unchanging static portfolio.

The final section examines the general issues associated with each of the differing dynamic and static portfolio management strategies. Empirical evidence from this book is combined with theory from literature on the topic, and some conclusions are drawn on the factors driving an effective portfolio management strategy.

2 Data Selection

Three different types of financial data are used as the dataset for this book; equities (stocks and shares); commodities; and risk-free assets. The choice of these three types of data serves several purposes. First, they represent the various main types of investment available to a prospective market investor. Equities represent assets relating to subsections of a particular market (e.g. a gas company, or an agri-business company); commodities represents the assets of an entire market (e.g. natural gas, or sugar); and a risk-free rate asset can be used as a proxy for the state of the overall economy and general market or macroeconomic trends. Second, these three types of data are far simpler to deal with and analyse than more complicated financial derivatives instruments, such as forwards or futures for example. And third, the risk-free rate of return, equities, and commodities data will all be required to examine portfolio management strategies. The inclusion of a risk-free rate allows for the calculation of the Sharpe ratio portfolio performance evaluation tool, while using both equities and commodities data allows for a comparison of their individual performance.

All of the data used in this book comes from the US financial markets. Equities are represented by the S&P

500, also known as Standard and Poor's 500, a leading market index containing 500 stocks from the NYSE or NASDAQ with a large market capitalization (the market's opinion of a firm's net worth). Using an index has two main benefits, and the inclusion of 500 diverse stocks removes the risk of the analysis being misled by events which may hit a few unrepresentative individual stocks. An index also allows for equities to be represented effectively by a single variable to facilitate easier and simpler analysis.

Commodities are represented using the S&P GSCI index, formerly known as the Goldman Sachs Commodities Index. Like the S&P 500 the S&P GSCI is also owned and published by the financial services company Standard and Poor's, but while the former contains 500 equities the S&P GSCI only contains 24 commodities. But these are taken across all commodity sectors to ensure diversity and balance out any effects which may affect only one or two sectors, and using the GSCI index in analysis therefore offers similar benefits to those just noted for the S&P 500 index.

The third variable used for this book's dataset is the US Treasury Bill rate, which represents the risk-free rate of return here. The US T-bill is backed by the US government and this backing ensures it is considered the least risky of all assets, and essentially risk-free as the T-bill rate would only fail to be paid in the unlikely event that the entire US government lost its ability to do so. A US T-bill interest rate also functions as a general indicator of macroeconomic trends and market conditions. In better (bullish) economic conditions with rising prices interest rates (including the US T-bill rate) will tend to be higher, as the government attempts to encourage saving and control spending and inflation. In worse (bearish) economic conditions with falling prices interest rates such as the US T-bill rate will tend to be lower, as government attempts to lower the cost of borrowing to stimulate spending to get the economy back on track.

Only three variables are used for the book's dataset. This keeps the analysis simpler, saves time, and allows for a greater focus on the three variables which have been selected. And this suits the primary aim of this book, which is to provide a detailed insight into the methods and applications of applied econometrics.

In terms of the specific datasets chosen, for those who wish to download the same data and replicate the analysis in this book, the S&P 500 is represented here by the 'S&P 500 Composite – Price Index' (S&PCOMP); the S&P GSCI data comes from the 'S&P GSCI Commodity Spot – Price Index' (CGSYSPT); and the US T-bill data is represented by the 'US Treasury Bill Rate' (USI60C..).

Monthly data is used for all three variables over the course of a 12 year sample, with 144 monthly data values for each type of asset over the period 1/4/1998 to

31/3/2010, the 1st of April 1998 to the 31st of March 2010. Monthly data was chosen over daily or weekly data due to a desire to incorporate a number of years into the sample, so that both upturns and downturns would be represented, without having to deal with hundreds or thousands of data values. A sample of exactly twelve years was chosen to allow the data to be used to give annual values, for yearly analysis over a prolonged period. And the specific choice of dates was made to allow an analysis of the 2007-8 global financial crisis and the period shortly afterwards, as will be explained in the portfolio strategy sections later. But price analysis of the sample datasets comes first, and this is the subject of the next section.

3 Price Analysis

3.1 Data Distribution

The first step of econometric analysis is to take natural logs of the raw S&PCOMP, CGSYSPT, and USI60C data for the S&P 500 equities index, S&P GSCI commodities index, and US Treasury Bill risk-free rate respectively. This can be easily done by creating a new column of data in a spreadsheet which applies the method '=LN(…)' to each original value of raw data, where '…' represents the original data value.

The process of taking natural logs is important as assets in financial markets are thought to follow a lognormal distribution, with values skewed to the right and a lower bound of zero (Brooks, 2008). Without this step a normal distribution would be implicitly assumed to hold for the data, with a zero skew and with both positive and negative values possible and equally as likely. But empirical evidence suggests that financial assets tend to be right (positive) skewed and not zero skewed, and that zero tends to be the lowest a stock or commodity price or the T-bill rate will go. While there are exceptions to this for T-bill rates they are rare, and even negative T-bill rates tend to be only just below zero to ensure that a lognormal distribution is the most applicable in practice.

With natural logs (L) taken of the equities, commodity and risk-free rate data the most useful next step is to give a visual representation of the results. This can reveal if any trends are immediately apparent in the data distribution, and can give an indication on where to proceed next. The following two diagrams graph the natural logs of the S&P 500 equities index data, denoted as LS&P500, and the S&P GSCI commodities index data, denoted as LGSCI.

S&P 500 and S&P GSCI monthly prices, 1998-2010

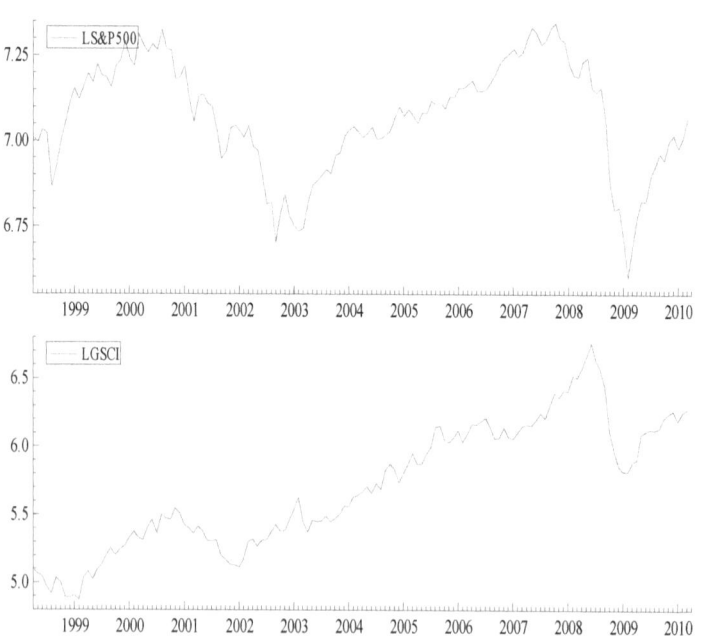

Some patterns are immediately visible after only a quick glance at the two graphs. The LS&P500 equities monthly data shows a general trend of peaks and troughs over the twelve year sample from 1/4/1998 to 31/3/2010, as equities prices rise and fall, rise and fall, and then rise again. The LGSCI commodities data shows a general trend of rising monthly prices over the same period, although there are smaller trends of falling prices in amongst this. While there are notable differences between the two graphs they both have one thing in common, and in both cases prices tend to move around over time as opposed to staying close to a particular value.

The next diagram graphs the natural logs of the US T-bill risk-free rate monthly data, denoted as LUSTRBILL.

US Treasury bill monthly rates, 1998-2010

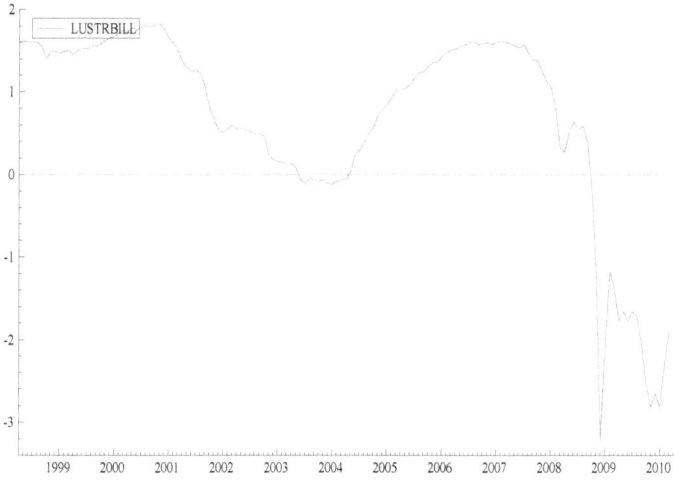

A glance at this graph reveals another general trend, and the period 1998-2010 was generally associated with declining monthly US Treasury bill risk-free rates, although there were smaller trends with rising rates in amongst this. Just like the other two graphs US T-bill values over the period show a trend of significant changes. Although all three of the graphs examined have different patterns, one with generally rising values (LGSCI), another with generally falling values (LUSTRBILL), and the third with peaks and troughs (LS&P500), all of the graphs see significant movements in values over time. And this has important implications for econometric analysis as the next section explains.

3.2 Stationarity, and Autocorrelation

If the value of equities prices, commodities prices, or US Treasury bill rates changes significantly over time, as the last section suggested, then the means and variances of these prices or rates will of course also change over time. This is a problematic result for econometric analysis as it means that an econometric regression, which is based around finding a mean and variance for a set of data, would not be applicable out of sample for a different time period, a situation known as a spurious regression. And therefore all of the insights associated with an economic regression would also not be applicable out of sample. In simple terms it is not possible to conduct econometric analysis, the purpose of this book, if data values deviate significantly from a certain level over time.

Data which stays close to a particular value over time is known as stationary data, and data which doesn't stay close to a particular value over time (as suggested by the three graphs earlier) is known as non-stationary data. If data is non-stationary then it is referred to as having a unit root, the term referring to the idea that an event which affects prices or rates (the root) grows outwards over time and has lasting effects which change the base value of the data. A unit root test can be performed to determine which of these two scenarios applies to the datasets used in this

17

book, but first it is useful to see a visual representation of the data's stationary or non-stationary qualities.

The following graphs show autocorrelation functions (ACF) and partial autocorrelation functions (PACF) for the S&P 500 equities, S&P GSCI commodities, and US T-bill risk-free rate data. An autocorrelation function (ACF) shows a variable's correlation with itself over time, from period to period. And a partial autocorrelation function (PACF) shows the correlation between a variable's value k periods ago and the current value of a variable, controlling for lags in the intermediate period. As a reminder these tests and all others in this book are not performed on the original equities, commodities and risk-free rate raw data downloaded from a data source, but the natural logs of the original data, for reasons explained in the last chapter.

144 monthly ACF and PACF values for each variable over the 1/4/1998 to 31/3/2010 sample period may be a few too many to examine visually, and therefore a decision was made to perform annual ACF and PACF tests for each variable instead. The result is 12 ACF and PACF annual values for each of the equities, commodities and risk-free rate data. In the graphs the lighter or red coloured bars relate to the ACF autocorrelation functions, and the darker or blue bars relate to the PACF partial autocorrelation functions. The first graph relates to the LS&P500 data, the graph below it is for the LGSCI data, and the final graph of the three is for the LUSTRBILL data.

Annual ACF and PACF for S&P 500 and S&P GSCI prices, 1998-2010

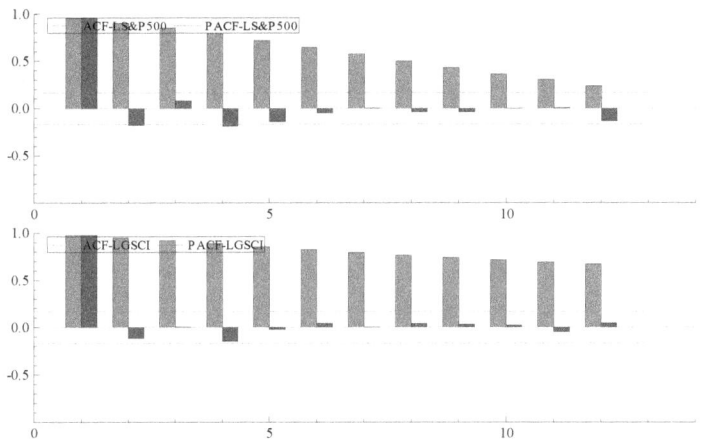

Annual ACF and PACF for US Treasury bill rates, 1998-2010

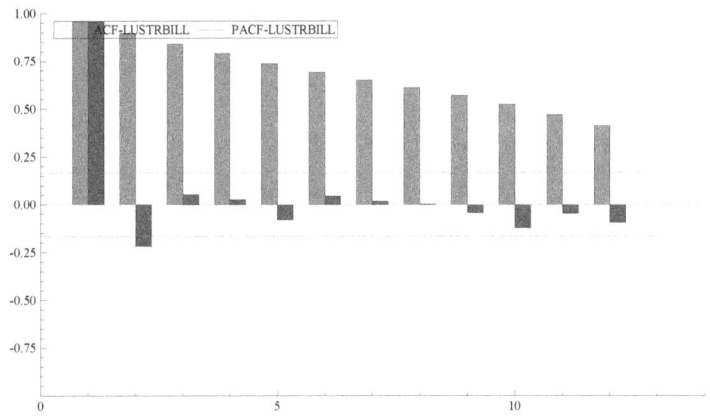

All three of the diagrams have a set of parallel horizontal bars, a little above and below the 0.0 level, and these represent the statistically acceptable levels of correlation. If a vertical autocorrelation function (ACF) bar or partial autocorrelation function (PACF) bar is within these parallel horizontal bars then autocorrelation or partial autocorrelation respectively may not be present. But if an ACF or PACF bar proceeds beyond the range shown by the parallel bars then statistically significant autocorrelation or partial autocorrelation respectively may occur. With this in mind it becomes possible to assess the three graphs together, as they all exhibit the same basic trend. Apart from the first bar (year one) the darker or blue PACF vertical bars always either stay within the statistically acceptable range denoted by the horizontal parallel bars, or if they do proceed beyond the parallel bars they are at least very close to being within this range. On the other hand all twelve of the lighter or red coloured ACF bars are outside of the statistically acceptable range denoted by the horizontal parallel bars, often by a significant margin, for all three of the variables.

An evaluation of the results suggested by the three graphs suggests that partial autocorrelation (PACF) is not really a problem for any of the S&P 500 equities, S&P GSCI commodities, or US Treasury bill risk-free rate of return variables. However, autocorrelation (ACF) is an issue for all three of these variables, and the value of a variable in one period is strongly correlated with the value of that variable in the next period. This presence of autocorrelation result holds even though the evaluation periods are measured in years, although the level of autocorrelation does appear to decline over time as the ACF bars become less steep toward the right side of the graphs. The fact that all of the ACF bars stretch too far above the statically acceptable levels for autocorrelation, as opposed to too far below the statistically acceptable levels, also reveals that it is positive autocorrelation and not negative autocorrelation which is present in this data. This means that data values tend to have a positive relationship with each other from period to period, and tend to follow on from each other in a trend, as opposed to repelling each other and heading in the opposite direction from the last data value in a volatile pattern, which would be negative autocorrelation.

Returning back to the issue of stationary or non-stationary data, the three annual ACF and PACF graphs for the LS&P500, LGSCI and LUSTRBILL data suggest that all of the data here is non-stationary and therefore problematic. The positive autocorrelation result confirms that trends are present in data values, as suggested earlier by the visual appearance of monthly prices, and that a shock to price values has a lasting and prolonged effect. This course suggests non-stationary data. For data to be stationary it must remain close to and fluctuate around a particular level, while trends in data values represents the opposite and involve movement away from a particular level. However, before any firm conclusions can be drawn on the non-stationary nature of the datasets, and possible solutions examined, a formal unit root test for stationarity is required. This is the topic of the next section.

3.3 Unit Root Test

Before a unit root test for stationary or non-stationary data can be performed a hypothesis must first be put forward, to clarify what exactly is being tested and how results will be assessed. The null hypothesis (H0), the theory which is to be tested, is that the datasets here are non-stationary and contain a unit root. Specifically, the null hypothesis is that a data value (y) at time period t (y_t) equals a data value in the previous time period (y_{t-1}), plus the random error variance (u_t) for time period t (i.e. there is autocorrelation). As the null hypothesis states that there is a clear one to one relationship between a data value at time t and the data value in the previous time period, after accounting for random variance error, the null hypothesis (H0) can be written as: $y_t = \varphi y_{t-1} + u_t$ where (Greek letter fi) $\varphi = 1$.

An alternate hypothesis (HA) is always tested alongside the null hypothesis, and the HA in this case is that the datasets here are stationary and do not contain a unit root. In the alternative hypothesis the equation $y_t = \varphi y_{t-1} + u_t$ is the same as before but the value of Greek letter fi is lower and $\varphi < 1$. The alternative hypothesis basically states that there is not a clear 1 to 1 relationship between data values from period to period, and that any relationship is too weak to allow conclusions to be drawn (i.e. there is no autocorrelation).

An augmented Dickey-Fuller (ADF) unit root test can be performed on the datasets to test for stationarity using econometric software. The ADF values provided by this test are then compared to critical values from statistical tables to determine the result of the hypothesis test. To find the relevant and correct critical values here three details must be taken into account. First, there is only one explanatory variable in the equation for each data variable, and this is the previous period's data value, $y_t = \varphi y_{t-1} + u_t$. Second, while there are visible trends in all of the datasets the LS&P500, LGSCI and LUSTRBILL data values each exhibit different trends with both rising and falling prices/rates (as noted in section 3.1), and therefore a 'without trend' ADF test is the most relevant choice. This leaves the data as it is, while an ADF 'with trend' model may assume a trend in one direction only and therefore give a less accurate critical value. Finally, six month lags in the data are chosen to be applied to the ADF test. This should be more than long enough for a past shock to stop having a major effect on future values if data is stationary, and any lingering shock effects beyond this length of time is likely to signal non-stationary data and a unit root.

With the previous time period's data value as the only explanatory variable, no trend, and six month lags on 144 monthly data values for each of the equities, commodities, and risk-free rate datasets, the critical values from statistical tables and the ADF test values are as follows:

Augmented Dickey-Fuller unit root test on LS&P 500 and LGSCI prices, and LUSTRBILL rates

Null hypothesis, H0: Series contains a unit root, $\varphi = 1$ where $y_t = \varphi y_{t-1} + u_t$ **Alternate hypothesis, HA:** Series doesn't contain unit root, $\varphi < 1$ with $y_t = \varphi y_{t-1} + u_t$		
Critical values	5% = -2.883	1% = -3.479
LS&P500 ADF	-2.46	
LGSCI ADF	-1.433	
LUSTRBILL ADF	-0.1109	

Using a 5% significance level (5% margin of error) the critical value for the augmented Dickey-Fuller (ADF) test is -2.883 for each of the three data variables according to statistical tables. And the most stringent 1% significance level (1% margin of error) gives a critical value of -3.479 from statistical tables. If the calculated ADF test result is lower (i.e. a larger negative number) than a critical value from statistical tables then the null hypothesis above is rejected, giving credence to the alternative hypothesis and the idea that data is stationary with no unit root. But if the ADF test result is not lower in value than the critical value from statistical tables then the null hypothesis cannot be rejected, and data is non-stationary with a unit root.

ADF values for the three 1/4/1998 to 31/3/2010 sample period datasets shows that all three contain a unit root, and the null hypothesis of non-stationary data cannot be rejected for any of them. The ADF test value for the LS&P500 equities price data is calculated at -2.46, the ADF for the LGSCI commodities price data is -1.433, and the ADF value for the LUSTRBILL risk-free rate data is -0.1109. None of these three values are lower (i.e. larger negative numbers) than even the 5% significance level critical value of -2.833, never mind the more stringent 1% significance level critical value of -3.479. It appears that the only way for the datasets here to become stationary, which is required in order to analyse them properly, is if the significance level (percentage margin of error tolerated) is raised above the standard maximum of 5% to give a lower critical value from statistical tables. And if the only way for the datasets here to be suitable is to allow greater error then there is clearly a problem.

With non-stationary datasets it appears that econometric analysis will be impossible here, but there is actually an established method to make non-stationary datasets stationary. The process involves making one change to the datasets, and this is the subject of the next section.

3.4 Differenced Data

When datasets are found to be non-stationary the next step is typically to 'difference' the data as many times as it takes to achieve the goal of stationary data. As the name suggests the process involves replacing data values with the difference between data values. For example, the original stationary data may have five values: (i) 7; (ii) 12; (iii) 4; (iv) 6; (v) 3. Differencing the data once would create a new dataset with four new values: (i) 5; (ii) -8; (iii) 2; (iv) -3. If this created stationary data then the process would end there and this would be the new dataset, but if the data was still non-stationary and with a unit root then it would have to be differenced for a second time, to create three new data values: (i) -13; (ii) 10; (iii) -5. And if this data was non-stationary it would require a third differencing process, to create two new values: (i) 23; and (ii) -15, and so on until the requirement of stationary data is met. Each time data is differenced the number of values drops by one, but with relatively large datasets used in practice (unlike this example) this won't change results.

Returning to the LS&P500, LGSCI, and LUSTRBILL data, each of the datasets was differenced (D) once to create new DL&P500, DLGSCI, and DLUSTRBILL data. This sees price and interest rate data become return data (i.e. period to period price or interest rate changes). With

27

this step complete the augmented Dickey-Fuller (ADF) unit root test introduced in the last section is run again, to determine whether the new differenced data still exhibits unwanted non-stationary characteristics. Results follow.

Dickey-Fuller unit root test on S&P 500 and S&P GSCI price changes, US T-bill rate changes

Null hypothesis, H0: Series contains a unit root. $\varphi = 1$ where $y_t = \varphi y_{t-1} + u_t$ Alternate hypothesis, HA: Series doesn't contain unit root. $\varphi < 1$ with $y_t = \varphi y_{t-1} + u_t$		
Critical values	5% = -2.883	1% = -3.479
DLS&P 500 ADF	-3.869**	
DLGSCI ADF	-5.123**	
DLUSTRBILL ADF	-4.691**	

The critical values for the ADF test are unchanged, and at -2.883 for the 5% significance level (5% margin of error), and at -3.479 for the more stringent 1% significance level (only 1% margin of error). As before the ADF test results must be lower (i.e. larger negative numbers) to reject the null hypothesis that the data is non-stationary and with a unit root. But this time the results are different, and all datasets are stationary as the null hypothesis is rejected in all cases. This is symbolized with the two stars next to each ADF result, and one star represents a rejection of the null hypothesis at the 5% level, while a second star represents a rejection of the null hypothesis at the 1% level. The DLS&P500 ADF value of -3.869, the DLGSCI ADF value of -5.123, and the DLUSTRBILL ADF value of -4.691 are all larger negative numbers than even the most stringent 1% significance level critical value of -3.479. This suggests that differencing the price and interest rate data just once is enough to achieve stationary data.

Having examined the appearance of (non-stationary) LS&P500 and LGSCI prices and LUSTRBILL interest rates in graphs before the differencing process, it is worth contrasting this with the new (stationary) returns data.

Monthly T-bill rate changes (returns), 1998-2010

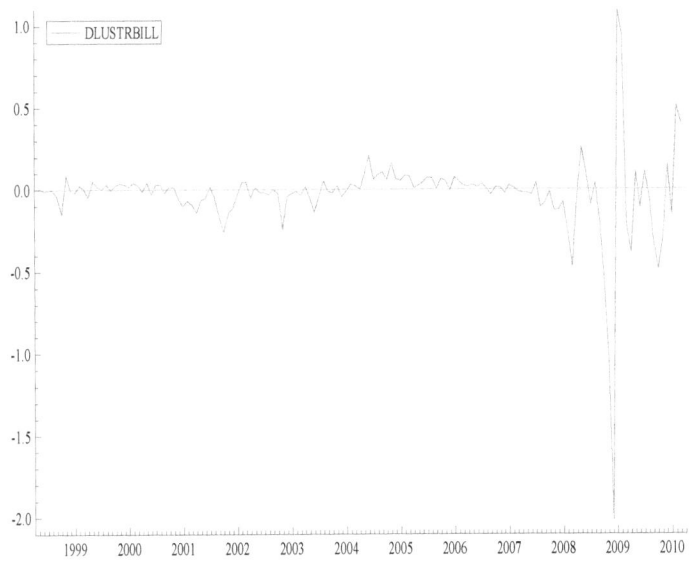

US Treasury bill interest rate changes (i.e. returns) show a very different pattern to the earlier interest rate data. After the differencing process the data now doesn't exhibit any upward or downward trends, but is instead centred on a zero level represented by the horizontal line. There are still fluctuations but the data values appear to always revert back to this level, exhibiting stationarity.

S&P 500 and S&P GSCI monthly price changes (returns), 1998-2010

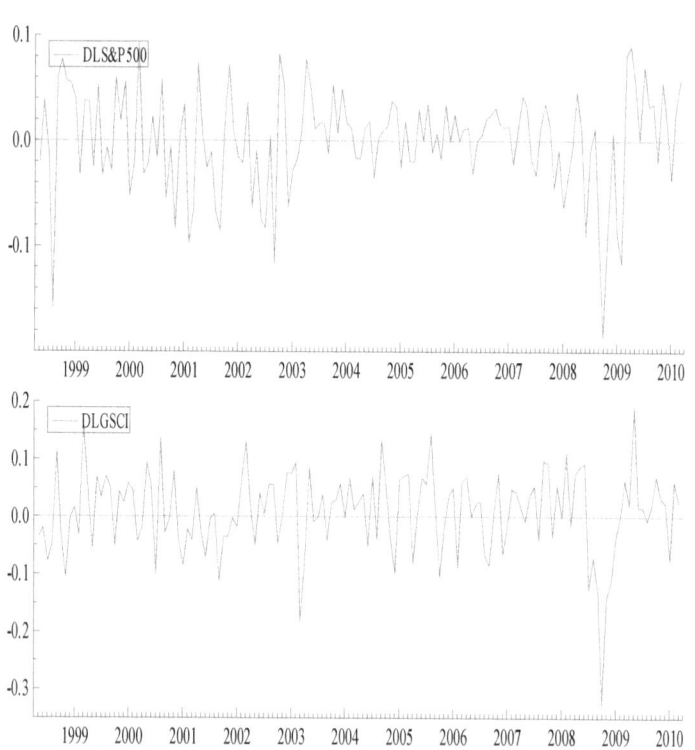

And a similar pattern appears to hold for both the S&P 500 and GSCI price change (returns) data too. The upward and downward trends visible in the original data before differencing (D) are now gone, and while there are still fluctuations data values appear to always revert back to this same level of roughly zero, to highlight stationarity. This is evident by the number of times that the data value trend line (the zigzag line) crosses the horizontal zero line in both the upper DLS&P500 and lower DLGSCI graphs.

Stationary data should also mean that there is no (or statistically insignificant) autocorrelation in the datasets. Autocorrelation function (ACF) and partial autocorrelation function (PACF) tests were run again on the new returns data to test this, and the results are in the following graphs.

Annual ACF, PACF for US T-bill returns, 1998-2010

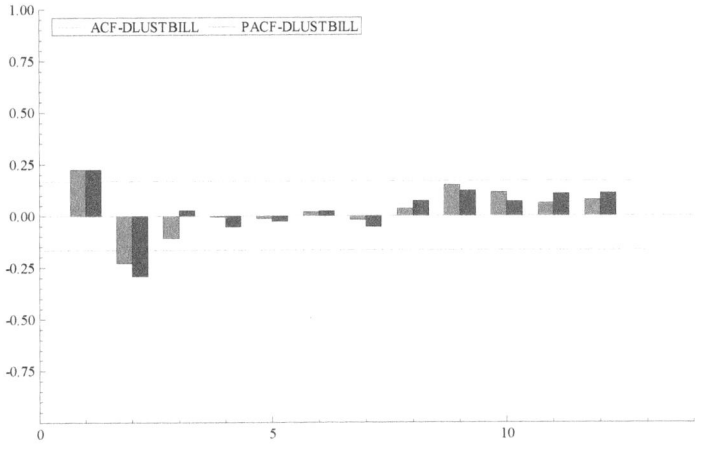

Annual ACF and PACF for S&P 500 and S&P GSCI returns, 1998-2010

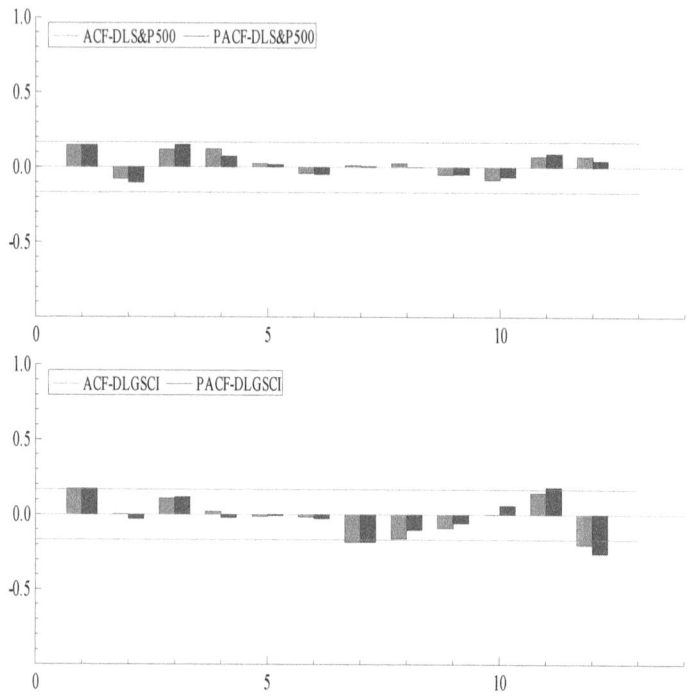

As before autocorrelation (ACF) is represented by the lighter or red vertical bars, and partial autocorrelation (PACF) is shown with the darker or blue coloured bars. The area between the parallel horizontal bars represents the region of statistical insignificance and acceptability, but if an ACF or PACF vertical bar proceeds either above or below this range then this suggests that autocorrelation or partial autocorrelation may be a statistically significant problem.

Looking at the three graphs for the 1/4/1998 to 31/3/2010 sample period reveals that, as expected, neither autocorrelation nor partial autocorrelation is a major problem with the newly differenced data. In the second graph for the S&P 500 data all twelve pairs of annual ACF and PACF bars are within the statistical insignificance zone denoted by the parallel horizontal bars. The first graph for US T-bills sees ten of the twelve pairs of vertical bars within the parallel bars, with only the first two sets of annual data a little beyond it. And the third graph for the GSCI data again sees most ACF and PACF annual bars within the acceptable zone, with only a few marginally over the line, and the last year's PACF value a little further past it. Although some of the ACF and PACF results are beyond the zone of statistical acceptability for the GSCI or US T-bill data this tends to be marginal, and an exception to the general trend of no statistically significant autocorrelation which exists in the differenced data.

Differencing the LS&P500, LGSCI, and LUSTRBILL data just once appears to have created the stationary data which further analysis will require. However, it is not only the stationarity of individual data sets which is important. The stationarity or otherwise of the relationship between datasets is also a factor which can affect econometric analysis, and this is looked at in the next section.

3.5 Cointegration Tests and Correction

The number of times that data must be differenced to ensure stationary data is known as the order of integration. If a linear combination of two or more integrated variables has a lower order of integration than the variables individually, then the variables are cointegrated (Brooks, 2008). Looking at the equities, commodities and risk-free datasets, the last section revealed that the LS&P500, LGSCI, and LUSTRBILL datasets must be differenced a single time to ensure stationary data, and they therefore have an order of integration of 1. And therefore if a linear combination of the LS&P500, LGSCI and LUSTRBILL data has an order of integration of 0, and is already stationary and doesn't need to be differenced at all, then the variables will be cointegrated.

If cointegration is defined as a stationary relationship between integrated variables, cointegration essentially means that the error term in an integrated variable regression model is stationary. In other words there is no error term at all for the regression, as error will always be at the same level (i.e. stationary) even as variables take on extreme values (as they are integrated and non-stationary), and error which is always the same and predictable is not error. Cointegration therefore means that regression error always equal zero. But while this may be true for the average long-run equilibrium it will of course not be true in practice for the short-run, where there will always be fluctuations and random error. Therefore the problem with cointegrated variables is that they result in an inaccurate model which contradicts reality. If this all appears too complicated to understand then there is an easier way of understanding why cointegration is a problem, which is to simply say that individual datasets have a different order of integration than the relationships between those different datasets, which creates imbalances and contradictions in econometric analysis.

With cointegration noted as a possible problem the next step is to test for it try and resolve it if necessary. There are a number of ways to do this, and one such method is known as the Engle-Granger Two-Step Method.

Engle-Granger Two-Step Method – Step 1

The first step of the Engle-Granger Two-Step Method sees a regression run on non-stationary variables, then a unit root test is performed on the regression's residuals (i.e. the error term in the regression). The LS&P500 dataset was regressed on the LGSCI and LUSTRBILL datasets to see the relationship between the three non-stationary variables over the 1/4/1998 to 31/3/2010 sample period, and the regression residuals are plotted in the following graph.

Residuals from regression of LS&P500 price data on LGSCI price data and LUSTRBILL rate data

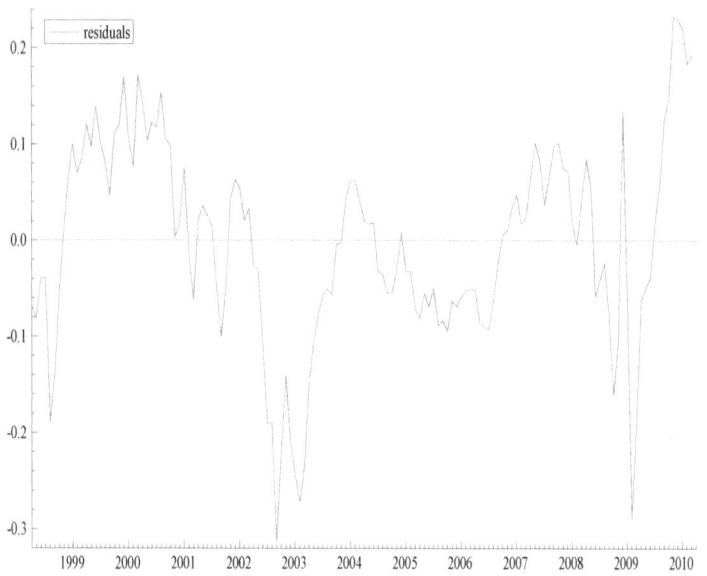

This graph appears to show conflicting results, and while the residual (i.e. error) values cross the average value (zero) horizontal line multiple times to suggest mean- reverting stationary data, there are also clear signs of upward or downward trends over time which may suggest non-stationary data and a unit root. A unit root test can reveal conclusively whether the residuals are stationary or non-stationary, and the following table shows the results of an augmented Dickey-Fuller (ADF) test on the regression residuals (error). This test follows the same principles of the earlier ADF tests, and again there is no trend or constant deterministic term (to avoid creating bias in results), but there are six month lags (enough time for past events to stop having an impact on current prices/rates, if data is stationary).

Dickey-Fuller unit root test on regression residuals

Null hypothesis, H0: Series contains a unit root. $\varphi = 1$ where $y_t = \varphi y_{t-1} + u_t$ Alternate hypothesis, HA: Series doesn't contain unit root. $\varphi < 1$ with $y_t = \varphi y_{t-1} + u_t$		
Critical values	5% = -1.942	1% = -2.581
Residuals ADF	-2.795**	

The critical value from statistical tables for the 5% significance level (5% margin of error tolerated) in the augmented Dickey-Fuller test is -1.942, and the critical value for the 1% significance level (only a 1% margin of error tolerated) is -2.581. Both of these are lower than the critical values seen in the earlier ADF tests, as each of those tests only applied to one variable and 144 monthly data values, while this ADF test applies to all three equities, commodities and risk-free variables and involves far more monthly data values. As the table suggests the ADF residuals value is -2.795, a lower number (larger negative number) than either critical value, and the null hypothesis is therefore rejected and the time series data for the regression error term does not contain a unit root and is stationary. The relationship between the LS&P500 equities data and the other datasets is therefore stationary, constant and predictable over time, and there is co-movement between the commodities, risk-free and equities data.

As a linear combination (i.e. a linear regression) of the integrated variables contains a lower order of integration than the variables themselves, and as the regression error term is stationary while the variables themselves are non-stationary, there is clear cointegration in the datasets. The implications of this can be seen by looking at both the graph and table above together. The Dickey-Fuller test result in the table suggest that the error term (residuals) is stationary over the length of the time series, and therefore (as explained earlier) error equals zero over the long-term. However, the graph shows that regression residuals (error) moves both up above and down below zero over short-term periods, and in the short-term the error term may therefore not be zero. This creates a situation where long-term error and short-term error don't match, and this naturally creates problems for the regression and for econometric analysis.

It's worth noting that the discovery of cointegration between equities (S&P 500) data and commodities (S&P GSCI) data here conflicts with studies done by others. Buyuksahin et al. (2008) find no co-movement and therefore no cointegration between equities and commodities assets, using a sample of data from January 1991 to May 2008. This suggests that cointegration test results may be highly dependent on the time period chosen for the sample data. This idea is supported by Buyuksahin et al. (2010) who note a period of correlation and co-movement between equities and commodities beginning in the late 1990s and then again from late 2008, which may explain why this book's 1998-2010 sample data found cointegration while the Buyuksahin et al. (2008) 1991-2008 data did not. But one benefit of finding cointegration in this book's sample data is that in leads on to the issue of resolving it, and this is the second step of the Engle-Granger Two-Step Method.

Engle-Granger Two-Step Method – Step 2

The second step of the Engle-Granger Two-Step Method attempts to resolve the problem of short-term error conflicting with long-term error, by correcting short-term deviations from the long-run cointegrated equilibrium through the use of an Error Correction Model (ECM). The ECM takes the regression from step 1 of the two step method, and then runs it again with differenced data and with the calculated residuals lagged one period. This is known as a cointegrating vector (Engle and Granger, 1987).

In the original regression of step 1 the LS&P500 time series data (y_t) was regressed on the LGSCI time series data (x_t) and LUSTRBILL time series data (w_t). This created the following regression model: $y_t = \beta_0 + \beta_1 x_t + \beta_2 w_t + u_t$, where β_0 is the constant/intercept term in the regression, β_1 is the coefficient value of the LGSCI term, β_2 is the coefficient value of the LUSTRBILL term, and u_t is the error term or residuals term. The Error Correction Model (ECM) with differenced data and calculated residuals lagged one period becomes: $\Delta y_t = \beta_0 + \beta_1 \Delta x_t + \beta_2 \Delta w_t + \beta_3 (y_{t-1} - \gamma_1 x_{t-1} + \gamma_2 w_{t-1}) + v_t$. Here Δ represents the change in a variable, v_t is the new error or residuals term for this amended model, and β_3 is the coefficient of the previously calculated residuals lagged one period. The ($y_{t-1} - \gamma_1 x_{t-1} - \gamma_2 w_{t-1}$) term is the previously calculated residual error (i.e. $u_t = y_t - x_t - w_t$ which rearranges the original equation $y_t = x_t + w_t + u_t$) after it is lagged one time period ($_{t-1}$), with γ_1 and γ_2 the coefficients for lagged calculated residuals for x_t and w_t respectively.

The calculated β_i coefficients for the ECM variables are given in the following table, along with t-values and p-values. The most important information in the table is the p-values, as these immediately reveal whether or not the variables are statistically significant. If a p-value is lower than the chosen significance level (typically 5% or 0.05, and for a more stringent test 1% or 0.01) in any test then the null hypothesis is rejected, but if the p-value is not lower than the significance level then the null hypothesis is not rejected. The null hypothesis here is H0: $\beta_i = 0$, or in other words the null hypothesis is that a variable's coefficient equals zero and the variable is therefore statistically insignificant. The alternative hypothesis is HA: $\beta_i \neq 0$, that a variable's coefficient does not equal zero and therefore the variable is statistically significant.

Error Correction Model (ECM) results for S&P 500 and S&P GSCI price changes, US T-bill rate changes

Error Correction Model, ECM:			
$\Delta y_t = \beta_0 + \beta_1 \Delta x_t + \beta_2 \Delta w_t + \beta_3(y_{t-1} - \gamma_1 x_{t-1} - \gamma_2 w_{t-1}) + v_t$			
Variable	Coefficient	T-value	P-value
Constant	-0.00143283	-0.360	0.720
DLGSCI	0.180170	3.16	0.002
DLUSTRBILL	-0.00852132	-0.534	0.594
Residuals_1	-0.0757872	-1.96	0.052

The DLGSCI variable (Δx_t) has a p-value of 0.002, and as this is lower than 0.01 the null hypothesis that $\beta_1 = 0$ is rejected at the most stringent 1% significance level (1% margin of error tolerated), and the DLGSCI variable is statistically significant in accordance with the ECM. However, the constant term has a p-value of 0.720, the DLUSTRBILL variable (Δw_t) has a p-value of 0.594, and the previously calculated residuals lagged one period denoted as residuals_1 ($y_{t-1} - \gamma_1 x_{t-1} - \gamma_2 w_{t-1}$) has a p-value at 0.052. As all three of these p-values exceed 0.05 or 5%, which is the maximum significance level usually tolerated for a hypothesis test, none of the individual null hypotheses that $\beta_0 = 0$, $\beta_2 = 0$ and $\beta_3 = 0$ can be rejected, and therefore the constant term, DLGSCI, and residuals_1 are all statistically insignificant. With these three important parameters all found irrelevant with the data here the Error Correction Model falls apart, and can't be used to resolve the cointegration problem in the datasets.

Brooks (2008) noted that the Error Correction Model has three problems which may make the model unworkable. (1) Unit root and cointegration results may not be robust if data samples are small in size. (2) If the causality between dependent and independent variables runs in both directions there may be a simultaneous equation bias, and if the regression of two variables had been reversed the results may have been different. (3) The ECM does not allow for a hypothesis test to be performed on the actual cointegration relationship between variables, and instead differenced and lagged data must proxy for it. The first problem here shouldn't explain why the ECM didn't work for the sample data here, as twelve years of monthly data should be a large enough sample size. But the second and especially third problems may explain why the ECM didn't work with the sample data here, and a multivariate model is therefore required to resolve these issues and deal with the cointegrated data.

Johansen Technique

Johansen (1991) devised a multivariate model which can be used to test for and resolve cointegration. The Johansen Technique is based on a vector autoregressive (VAR) model, which takes the original univariate autoregressive (AR) model where future values are estimated using the sum of weighted past values, and generalizes it to allow for more than one evolving variable. With a 'g' number of non-stationary (i.e. containing unit roots) variables thought to be cointegrated, a VAR model with a 'k' number of lags can be set up as in the following table. And to use the Johansen Technique this VAR model is turned into a Vector Error Correction Model (VECM) using the method given in the table.

Vector Autoregressive Model (VAR) and Vector Error Correction Model (VECM) results for the Johansen technique

Vector Autoregressive Model, VAR:				
$y_t \quad = \quad \beta_1 y_{t-1} \quad + \quad \beta_2 y_{t-2} \quad + \ldots + \quad \beta_k y_{t-k} \quad + \quad u_t$				
$g*1 \qquad g*g \;\; g*1 \qquad g*g \;\; g*1 \qquad\qquad g*g \;\; g*1 \qquad g*1$				
Vector Error Correction Model, VECM:				
$\Delta y_t \;\; = \;\; \Pi y_{t-k} + \Gamma_1 \Delta y_{t-1} + \Gamma_2 \Delta y_{t-2} + \ldots + \Gamma_{k-1} \Delta y_{t-(k-1)} + u_t$				
$\Pi = \Pi_1 + \ldots + \Pi_k - I;$ $\Gamma_i = \Pi_1 + \ldots + \Pi_i - I \qquad$ (where i = 1,…,k-1)				

A vector autoregressive model (VAR) calculates the value of a dependent variable at time t (y_t) as the sum of the previous period's dependent variable value (y_{t-1}) given a certain weight (β_1), and the previous period's dependent variable value before that (y_{t-2}) given a specific weight (β_2), and so on, back 'k' lags to time period $_{t-k}$ (with y_{t-k} weighted at β_k), plus the error term (u_t). VAR: $y_t = \beta_1 y_{t-1} + \beta_2 y_{t-2} + \ldots + \beta_k y_{t-k} + u_t$. And with a 'g' number of non-stationary variables thought to be cointegrated, there is a g*1 number of dependent and lagged dependent variables (and by implication the error term), and a g*g number of coefficients (i.e. a coefficient matrix) for the lagged dependent variables as in the above table.

The Vector Error Correction Model (VECM) calculates the change in a dependent variable (Δy_t), and a 'g' number of differenced variables are calculated using a similar method to that just explained for the VAR. Three predictable changes are made to turn the VAR into the VECM; and first the lagged dependent variables change from y_{t-1}, y_{t-2} etc. to the differenced versions Δy_{t-1}, Δy_{t-2} etc. Second, a new set of coefficients are created to go along with these new lagged variables as β_1, β_2, etc. are replaced with Γ_1, Γ_2, etc. (i.e. a new set of Greek letters, here denoted with capital Gamma). Third, the number of lags is reduced from 'k' to 'k-1' as one period is lost in the differencing process (e.g. differencing a sample of 100 time series values creates 99 time series differences values), and the final lagged variable is from time $_{t-(k-1)}$, with its corresponding coefficient set at $_{k-1}$. These three predictable changes give the equation $\Delta y_t = \Gamma_1 \Delta y_{t-1} + \Gamma_2 \Delta y_{t-2} + \ldots + \Gamma_{k-1} \Delta y_{t-(k-1)} + u_t$, but one additional and bigger change to the VAR model is also required to give VECM: $\Delta y_t = \Pi y_{t-k} + \Gamma_1 \Delta y_{t-1} + \Gamma_2 \Delta y_{t-2} + \ldots + \Gamma_{k-1} \Delta y_{t-(k-1)} + u_t$. The addition of a Πy_{t-k} term completes the change from a VAR model to the VECM, where $\Pi = \Pi_1 + \ldots + \Pi_k - I$, and I gives the order of integration. The Π term is a long-run coefficient matrix, and the Johansen cointegration test calculates the rank of the Π matrix by examining the number of its characteristic roots, known as eigenvalues, which are different from zero (Brooks, 2008).

Returning back to the LS&P500, LGSCI, and LUSTRBILL datasets, all three were inserted into the VECM as dependent (y_t) variables, with the US T-bill data arranged first to reveal any cointegrating relationship between the equities and commodities indices. But before any cointegrating relationship can be examined a cointegration test is required. There are two possible types of Johansen cointegration test, one based on a trace test where the null hypothesis is that the rank of the Π matrix is less than or equal to ($\leq$) a certain number, while the other type is based on an eigenvalue test where the null hypothesis is that the rank of the Π matrix is equal to ($=$) a certain number. The former will be used here, and hypothesis tests will be based on the results of a trace test.

The cointegration test has three different null hypotheses (H0), each with a different alternative hypothesis (HA) based on the hypothesised rank of the Π matrix:

(1) H0: Rank ≤ 0; HA: Rank $= 1$;

(2) H0: Rank ≤ 1; HA: Rank $= 2$;

(3) H0: Rank ≤ 2; HA: Rank $= 3$.

As explained earlier if the calculated p-value for a test is lower than the chosen significance level (typically 5% for a 5% margin of error, or 1% for the most stringent 1% margin of error) the null hypothesis is rejected, but if the p-value exceeds the chosen significance level then the null hypothesis cannot be rejected. With this in mind the test results can be presented in the following table with analysis of their implications following on afterwards.

Johansen cointegration test

Null hypotheses, H0: Rank ≤ 0; Rank ≤ 1; Rank ≤ 2. Alternate hypotheses, HA: Rank $= 1$; Rank $= 2$; Rank $= 3$			
H0: Rank $\leq$	HA: Rank $=$	Trace test	P-value
0	1	1039.5	[0.000]**
1	2	8.4653	[0.784]
2	3	1.8138	[0.808]

In the first row the null hypothesis (H0) is that the Π rank ≤ 0, but with a p-value of 0.000 this is rejected. The two stars next to the p-value signify that the null hypothesis is rejected at both the 5% (first star) and the most stringent 1% (second star) significance level. With H0 rejected the alternative hypothesis (HA) that the rank = 1 gains support, but no firm conclusions can be drawn until the other rows' hypothesis tests are also examined.

The second row has the null hypothesis that the Π rank $\leq$ 1. And with a p-value at 0.784, above 0.05 which signifies a 5% significance level, this null hypothesis cannot be rejected. This support for the null hypothesis in the second row naturally provides evidence against the alternative hypothesis in the second row, HA: rank = 2.

Finally, the third row's null hypothesis is that the Π rank $\leq$ 2. And with the third row p-value at 0.808, above 0.05 and a 5% significance level, this null hypothesis can't be rejected. This result in turn casts doubt on the alternative hypothesis in the third row, that the Π rank = 3.

Putting the results together, there is strong evidence supporting the first row alternative hypothesis of HA: Π rank = 1; second row null hypothesis H0: Π rank $\leq$ 1; and third row null hypothesis of H0: Π rank $\leq$ 2. And there is strong evidence against the first row null hypothesis of H0: Π rank $\leq$ 0; second row alternative hypothesis HA: Π rank = 2; and third row alternative hypothesis of HA: Π rank = 3. Combining all of these findings can only result in one possible conclusion, that the Π matrix rank = 1, and there is only one cointegrating vector present in the datasets.

With only one cointegrating vector (cointegration of order 1) present in the datasets the solution to the problem of cointegration is relatively straightforward. Remember that cointegration is defined as the situation where any linear relationship between two or more variables has a lower order of integration than the variables individually. Therefore resolving the problem of cointegration simply requires taking steps to ensure that both the individual variables and a linear relationship between them have the same order of integration.

In the case of the data here the LS&P500, LGSCI and LUSTRBILL datasets were found to contain integration of order 1 (i.e. they each had to be differenced one time in order to achieve stationary data), while in the Engle-Granger test earlier a Dickey-Fuller test revealed that a relationship between these same integrated variables was already stationary (i.e. integration of order 0). The reason the relationship between the integrated variables is stationary is because there is a predictable co-movement between the variables, which counteracts their individual non-stationary qualities. But if this co-movement was removed then the integration countering effect would also be removed, leaving a linear relationship between the LS&P500, LGSCI and LUSTRBILL data with the same order of integration as the variables individually, integration of order 1, and thereby eliminating the cointegration issue.

More details on the specifics of the co-movement between the integrated variables are required before it can be accurately removed. The following table reveals the cointegrating relationship between the LS&P500 equities index and the LGSCI commodities index relative to US T-bills (which can proxy for market conditions), after the VECM was run with differenced data.

Cointegrating relationship between price indices (S&P 500, S&P GSCI) and US T-bills, 1/4/1998 to 31/3/2010

Reduced form beta	
DLS&P500	2.8379
DLGSCI	-0.55557
Constant	-0.024141

The reduced form beta values for DLS&P500 and DLGSCI show the relationship between the two indices relative to US T-bills over the data sample period 1/4/1998 to 31/3/2010. And this relationship is the long-run solution to the problem of cointegration in the datasets, and can be used to adjust for co-movement in the data. This will be used later in the portfolio strategy section, but first the datasets will be examined again individually in the next section. With a solution found to the cointegration problem the differenced data calculated earlier can now be used without concern, and this turns prices and rates into returns, as price analysis becomes return analysis.

4 Return Analysis

4.1 AR and MA Processes

In the last chapter the LS&P500, LGSCI and LUSTRBILL datasets (i.e. natural logs of the original S&P500, S&P GSCI and US T-BILL data) were differenced a single time to make them stationary, creating new DLS&P500, DLGSCI and DLUSTRBILL returns datasets. With the requirement for stationary data met with these new datasets (and with cointegration addressed for later) the focus can now turn to finding the model which best suits the datasets, to offer the most explanatory power.

The Box-Jenkins (1976) method models time series data using what is known as an ARIMA method. The AR part of ARIMA stands for an autoregressive process, the I stands for the order of integration and the level of differencing required, and the MA stands for a moving average process. As the DLS&P500, DLGSCI and DLUSTRBILL datasets are already stationary and have an order of integration of 0 here the I in ARIMA equals 0, and it therefore disappears to leave just an ARMA model. This combines an AR (p) process and an MA (q) process, where the p and q describe the number of lagged time periods in the AR model or MA model respectively. In terms of the difference between the AR and MA models, and the reason why both are required, the AR model includes lagged dependent variables as its explanatory variables, while the MA model includes lagged error terms as its explanatory variables. The table below shows this.

Autoregressive (AR) and Moving Average (MA) processes

AR (p) process
$y_t = \varphi_0 + \varphi_1 y_{t-1} + \ldots + \varphi_p y_{t-p} + u_t$
MA (q) process   (assuming u_t is a white noise term with $E(u_t) = 0$ and $\mathrm{var}(u_t) = \sigma^2$)
$y_t = \Theta_0 + \Theta_1 u_{t-1} + \ldots + \Theta_q u_{t-q} + u_t$

An autoregressive (AR) process predicts time series data (y_t) using a constant term (φ_0, a long-term average), lagged time series data from previous periods (y_{t-1}, y_{t-2} etc. back to y_{t-p}) each weighted with their own coefficients (φ_1, φ_2 etc. back to φ_p), and the error term for the current period (u_t). And u_t has an expected value of 0 and a constant variance σ^2. The value of p determines the number of lags in the AR (p) process, and if p = 0 the AR (0) model is $y_t = \varphi_0 + u_t$, while if p = 3 the AR (3) model would be $y_t = \varphi_0 + u_t + \varphi_1 y_{t-1} + \varphi_2 y_{t-2} + \varphi_3 y_{t-3}$, and so on.

A moving average (MA) process predicts time series data (y_t) using a constant term (Θ_0, a long-term average), lagged error term data from previous periods (u_{t-1}, u_{t-2} etc. back to u_{t-p}) which are each weighted with their own corresponding coefficients (Θ_1, Θ_2 etc. back to Θ_p), and the error term for the current period (u_t). The value of q determines the number of lags in the MA (q) process, and if q = 0 the MA (0) model would be $y_t = \Theta_0 + u_t$, while if q = 2 the MA (2) model would be $y_t = \Theta_0 + u_t + \Theta_1 u_{t-1} + \Theta_2 u_{t-2}$, and so on.

In order to determine the optimum values of p and q which best fit the time series datasets here econometric calculations and analysis will be required. This takes place in the next section using the Akaike Information Criterion (AIC).

4.2 Akaike Information Criterion

The Akaike Information Criterion (AIC) can be used to determine the specific AR and MA processes which the time series data follow. The measure estimates the relative amount of information lost when a particular model is used, and in doing so reveals the goodness of fit of a model relative to alternative models. A lower AIC value signifies a superior model with a better goodness of fit and less information lost. Calculating the Akaike Information Criterion involves the formula: $AIC = 2K - 2Ln(L)$, where K = no. of parameters, L = maximized likelihood function value, and Ln = natural logarithm (Brooks, 2008).

Although more efficient than other methods, the Akaike Information Criterion is not without its flaws, and it tends to be inconsistent and biased toward a larger more complex model with more variables, a problem known as overfitting. But a couple of steps can be made to improve the AIC. First, the AIC value can be amended to correct for its bias, and an AICc (where c stands for correction) accounts for the number of time periods in a time series model, and effectively punishes the use of more lagged variables with smaller sample sizes. The modified AICc (univariate one variable) method is calculated as follows, where N is the number of data values:

$$AICc = AIC + [2K(K + 1) / (N - K - 1)]$$

In a second step to improve the AIC only lag lengths up to AR (4) and MA (4) will be tested, to further minimize the risk of overfitting with excess variables. The following table shows the results of the AICc test for the DLS&P500 data representing the S&P 500 variable.

ARMA AICc results for S&P 500 returns

DLS&P500					
	MA (0)	MA (1)	MA (2)	MA (3)	MA (4)
AR (0)	-456.70	-458.82	-458.379	-456.37	-457.56
AR (1)	-457.90	-458.69	-456.772	-457.06	-455.73
AR (2)	-457.40	-456.82	-454.69	-459.28	-458.12
AR (3)	-458.77	-457.48	-455.850	-454.33	-456.12
AR (4)	-457.69	-455.70	-453.86	-452.01	-451.70

As noted earlier a lower AIC value represents a superior model with less explanatory information lost, and a better goodness of fit for the data. The yellow or darkened cell here highlights the lowest value in the grid, at -459.28. And this value occurs with an AR (2) process and MA (3) process, otherwise known as an ARMA (2, 3) process, for the DLS&P500 dataset.

The next table shows the results of an AICc test for the DLGSCI dataset. As before the lowest value signals the most accurate and informative model for the data.

ARMA AICc results for S&P GSCI returns

DLGSCI					
	MA (0)	MA (1)	MA (2)	MA (3)	MA (4)
AR (0)	-344.13	-346.75	-344.93	-344.30	-342.95
AR (1)	-346.44	-345.22	-343.28	-342.70	-340.99
AR (2)	-344.55	-343.32	-341.74	-352.32	-346.64
AR (3)	-344.54	-342.59	-340.60	-350.65	-350.02
AR (4)	-342.60	-347.66	-346.16	-349.84	-348.46

In this grid the yellow or darkened cell with the lowest value has a value at -352.32. And just as with the previous AICc test for the DLS&P500 data, this AICc test for the DLGSCI data shows that the most applicable and best model with the least information lost follows an AR (2) process and an MA (3) process, also known as an ARMA (2, 3) process.

The final table below shows the results of the AICc test for the DLUSTRBILL dataset. In this case the lowest value, again highlighted by the yellow or darkened cell in the table, is 0.61924. But this time the lowest value, and the lowest information loss and best goodness of fit, is associated with an AR (2) process and an MA (4) process, otherwise known as an ARMA (2, 4) process.

ARMA AICc results for US T-bill returns

DLUSTRBILL					
	MA (0)	MA (1)	MA (2)	MA (3)	MA (4)
AR (0)	22.904	11.111	8.97989	8.19617	9.92101
AR (1)	17.515	11.103	9.27543	9.62731	11.9653
AR (2)	6.7729	8.6771	10.4064	11.6228	0.61924
AR (3)	8.7085	10.628	12.2839	13.3603	2.19421
AR (4)	10.300	12.236	14.1504	13.5634	3.30380

The ARMA models which best fit the S&P 500 equities index, S&P GSCI commodities index, and US Treasury bill risk-free rate of return variables have therefore been determined. The next section reveals the details of the specific characteristics of these models.

4.3 ARMA Models, Means and Volatility

It has been determined that an ARMA (2, 3) model best fits both the DLS&P500 and DLGSCI datasets, and an ARMA (2, 4) model best fits the DLUSTRBILL dataset. With this information it is now possible to create specific ARMA models complete with coefficient values for each of the variables, for the sample time period 1/4/1998 to 31/3/2010. These are presented in the following table.

ARMA (2, 3) models for S&P 500 returns and S&P GSCI returns, and ARMA (2, 4) US T-bill returns

DLS&P500	$y_t = 4.86820e\text{-}005 + 1.14888y_{t-1} - 0.818848y_{t-2} - 1.00329u_{t-1} + 0.613188u_{t-2} + 0.297381u_{t-3}$
DLGSCI	$y_t = 0.00766969 + 1.10700y_{t-1} - 0.744435y_{t-2} - 0.994195u_{t-1} + 0.641358u_{t-2} + 0.281196u_{t-3}$
DLUSTBILL	$y_t = -0.0236404 + 1.54907y_{t-1} - 0.682619y_{t-2} - 1.38135u_{t-1} + 0.0765492u_{t-2} + 0.444329u_{t-3} + 0.0329823u_{t-4}$

Mean return and return standard deviation (volatility, σ) values for each ARMA series return can also be calculated, and the results for the DLS&P500, DLGSCI and DLUSTRBILL data are given in the next table.

57

Mean and standard deviation volatility values for ARMA (2, 3) S&P 500 and S&P GSCI return models, and ARMA (2, 4) US T-bill returns

	Mean	SD volatility (σ)
DLS&P500	0.000353714	0.0455612
DLGSCI	0.00820923	0.0660869
DLUSTBILL	-0.0245214	0.22509

The values here will be used later on in the portfolio strategy section, but before that volatility models need to be determined for the three datasets. This is the subject of the next section.

5 Volatility Analysis

5.1 GARCH Model

In the last chapter ARMA models were used to represent the returns of the S&P 500, S&P GSCI and US T-bill datasets, but returns are not the only concern to an investor and the risk associated with those returns is just as important. This section will model the risk or volatility of returns, using GARCH to represent S&P 500, S&P GSCI and US T-bill datasets. GARCH stands for Generalized Autoregressive Conditionally Heteroscedasticity, and is a generalized version of an Autoregressive Conditionally Heteroskedastic model (ARCH). While an ARCH model explains the variance (volatility squared) of a model using only lagged error squared terms, a GARCH model adds lagged variance terms to this as shown in the table below.

GARCH model

GARCH model
$\sigma^2_t = \alpha_0 + \alpha_1 u^2_{t-1} + \ldots + \alpha_q u^2_{t-q} + \beta_1 \sigma^2_{t-1} + \ldots + \beta_p \sigma^2_{t-p}$
q = number of lagged error squared terms
p = number of lagged variance (volatility squared) terms

The first thing to note about the GARCH model is that it includes squared terms, unlike the ARMA model from the last section. This is done to remove the problems associated with positive and negative values cancelling each other out when dealing with volatility. While (for example) a positive return of 0.05 in one period (i.e. a profit) and negative return (i.e. a loss) of -0.05 in the next period does give an average return of 0, this is not true for volatility. Positive volatility (i.e. an upward trend) of 0.05 in one period and then negative volatility (i.e. a downward trend, actual negative volatility would of course be impossible as you can't take away volatility) of -0.05 in the next does not mean the average volatility was 0. There has still been volatility irrespective of the direction, and to account for this in a model and remove the negative signs it is common to square volatility values to create a variance value, from which a square root can be taken to give a volatility measure.

Looking at the GARCH model as a whole, it states that this period's variance (σ^2_t) equals a constant term (α_0, a long-term average), and lagged error squared terms (u^2_{t-1}, u^2_{t-2}, etc. back to u^2_{t-q}) each weighted with their respective coefficient (α_1, α_2, etc. back to α_q), and lagged variance terms (σ^2_{t-1}, σ^2_{t-2}, etc. back to σ^2_{t-p}) each weighted with their respective coefficient (β_1, β_2, etc. back to β_p). And the value of p gives the number of lagged variance terms, as the value of q describes the number of lagged error terms.

The GARCH model is considered to be more efficient than an ARCH model, and by adding lagged variance terms (known as fitted model variance) it is less likely to break non-negativity constraints (i.e. the requirement that parameters are not negative). Another advantage to using GARCH over ARCH is that it is essentially using the same type of model for return variance as was used in the last section for returns themselves. The ARMA model predicted returns using lagged dependent variable terms (of lag length p) and lagged error terms (of lag length q), and this GARCH model predicts return variance (volatility squared) using lagged dependent variable terms (of lag length p) and lagged error (squared) terms (of lag length q). Therefore the GARCH model could be seen as an ARMA model for the conditional variance (i.e. variance which is unknown and which depends upon other variables, such as lagged variance and lagged error terms).

5.2 AIC for GARCH

The Akaike Information Criterion (AIC) can be used to determine the optimum GARCH model to represent the return volatility of the datasets, just as it was used earlier to determine the most accurate ARMA model to represent the returns of the datasets. As before it will be the AICc value which is calculated, due to its advantages over the original AIC measure, and a lower AICc value signifies less information lost and a superior goodness of fit for a better model. and a But while the ARMA model was tested with values of $p = 0$, …, $p = 4$, and values of $q = 0$, …, $q = 4$, the GARCH model will only be tested with values of $p = 1$, …, $p = 4$, and values of $q = 1$, …, $q = 4$. The reason for this is that a value of $q > 0$ is a pre-requisite for the model, and it would break down with a value of $q = 0$, while a value of $p = 0$ would represent an ARCH model and not a GARCH model. And as was explained in the last section a GARCH model has many advantages over an ARCH model in representing return variance, especially having used an ARMA model to model returns.

GARCH return variance for the DLS&P500 returns time series dataset is presented in the following table. The table reveals that the lowest AICc value occurs with a GARCH (1, 4) model, with $p = 1$ and $q = 4$, and that this gives a value of -479.017. However, the cell which has been shaded a yellow or darkened colour to represent the superior GARCH model is not this cell but that at GARCH (1, 1), with the second lowest AICc value at -478.658. The reason that the second lowest value has been chosen over the lowest here is because the difference between them is so small (at 0.359), and it isn't worth 3 extra lagged variables (from $q = 1$ to $q = 4$) in a model just for this barely significant difference. This shows that model selection is not simply a case of finding the lowest number, and analysis needs to take place to determine if extra lags are worth it.

GARCH AICc results for S&P 500 return variance

DLS&P500			
	$q = 1$	$q = 2$	$q = 3$	$q = 4$
$p = 1$	-478.658	-478.587	-478.158	-479.017
$p = 2$	-476.658	-477.274	-476.76	-477.208
$p = 3$	-474.63	-475.274	-476.408	-475.329
$p = 4$	-472.63	-473.274	-474.409	-474.409

The small difference in AICc values between the lowest value model and one with fewer lags was not the only reason a GARCH (1, 1) model was preferred for the S&P 500 returns data however, and this idea was not mentioned in the last section for the ARMA models. Another reason for selecting a GARCH (1, 1) model for the DLS&P500 data is because of the GARCH results for the DLGSCI return variance time series data. The next table gives GARCH AICc values for the GSCI commodities data to explain more.

GARCH AICc results for S&P GSCI return variance

DLGSCI				
	q = 1	q = 2	q = 3	q = 4
p = 1	-350.74	-348.967	-346.965	-344.964
p = 2	-348.180	-347.783	-344.702	-342.702
p = 3	-346.978	-344.180	-343.867	###
p = 4	-344.978	###	###	###

In this table the '###' values mean that a result could not be calculated using econometric software. The lowest AICc value here, in the yellow or darkened cell, occurs with p =1 and q =1. And therefore a GARCH (1, 1) model is the best model for the DLGSCI dataset, with the lowest amount of information lost and the best goodness of fit. With a GARCH (1, 1) best for the GSCI commodities data there are advantages to also selecting it for the S&P 500 equities data, even though it is slightly worse than a GARCH (1, 4) model as just noted, and selecting the same model for both assets facilitates a more direct comparison later on in this book in the portfolio strategy section.

GARCH AICc values for the DLUSTRBILL dataset are given in the following table, with the yellow or darkened cell again highlighting the lowest value in the table. And this lowest value again indicates a superior model with the most accurate number of lagged variance terms and lagged error squared terms.

GARCH AICc results for US T-bill return variance

	q = 1	q = 2	q = 3	q = 4
DLUSTRBILL				
p = 1	-248.634	-247.987	-245.987	-244.133
p = 2	-254.357	-246.608	###	###
p = 3	-253.958	-252.297	-256.179	-248.593
p = 4	-252.787	-250.152	-248.831	###

The lowest value for the US T-bill return variance data is -256.179, and it occurs with a GARCH (3, 3) model, where $p = 3$ and $q = 3$. This suggests that the most accurate GARCH model for the US T-bill returns would have lagged variance terms going back three periods (as $p = 3$), and lagged error squared terms gong back three periods (as $q = 3$).

GARCH Model Variations

Although a GARCH (1, 1) model has just been selected as best for the DLS&P500 and DLGSCI data, and a GARCH (3, 3) model has been selected as best for the DLUSTRBILL data, further improvements may still be possible. There are variations of the standard GARCH model which may give a lower AICc value, and therefore represent a further reduction in the amount of information lost and a better goodness of fit for the datasets. Three possible variations of the original GARCH model are EGARCH, where E stands an exponential GARCH model; GJR-GARCH, where GJR stands for Glosten-Jagannathan-Runkle (the creators) and where asymmetric adjustment is added to the model; and GARCH-M, where the M stands for mean and where the model adds a heteroscedasticity term directly into the mean equation.

However, testing a range of additional GARCH models, for each of the three datasets, with every value of p and q from 1 to 4 (as before) would take a significant amount of time and space, and to avoid this only a GARCH (1, 1) model will be assessed (with p =1 and q = 1). This was the GARCH model chosen as best for both the DLS&P500 and DLGSCI datasets, and it makes sense for alternative GARCH variations to be tested on the same basis. And although the GARCH (1, 1) model was not the best type for the DLUSTRBILL data for US T-bills, the two equities and commodities indices are more important datasets for the purposes of econometric analysis, and the US T-bills dataset serves mainly as a proxy for market conditions and macroeconomic trends.

The calculated AICC results for GARCH (1, 1) variations EGARCH (1, 1), GJR-GARCH (1, 1), and GARCH-M (1, 1) are presented in the next table.

GARCH (1, 1) model types and their AICc results

GARCH (1,1) model type	DLS&P500 AICC	DLGSCI AICC	DLUSTBILL AICC
EGARCH	-491.348	-351.838	-261.163
GJR-GARCH	-481.879	###	-265.434
GARCH-M	-476.691	-353.97	-246.652

Looking first at the DLS&P500 AICc results (the first data column), the EGARCH (1, 1) model is the best of the three variations with the lowest value of -491.348 highlighted by the yellow or darkened cell. In terms of the DLGSCI GARCH model variations (data column two), the best model with the lowest amount of information lost is the GARCH-M (1, 1), with its -353.97 AICc value also in a yellow or darkened cell. And finally the DLUSTRBILL AICc data results (the third column) suggest that the best GARCH variation for US T-bills is the GJR-GARCH (1, 1), with the third column's lowest value of -265.434 in the yellow or darkened cell.

In order to determine whether any of these model variations are an improvement over the original GARCH model the AICc values for the three datasets with the alternative EGARCH, GJR-GARCH, and GARCH-M models need to be compared to the AICc values from the original model. The original lowest AICc value for the DLS&P500 data was -478.658, with a GARCH (1, 1) model, but the EGARCH (1, 1) model offers an improvement with the lower AICc value of -491.348. The original lowest AICc value for the DLGSCI data was -350.74, with a GARCH (1, 1) model, but the GARCH-M (1, 1) model variation gives a better goodness of fit with a lower AICc value of -353.97. And the original lowest AICc for the DLUSTRBILL dataset was -256.179, with a GARCH (3, 3) model, but the GJR-GARCH (1, 1) model variation is better with a lower AICc value of -265.434 to reduce the amount of lost information. The EGARCH, GARCH-M and GJR-GARCH model variations chosen above for each of the three datasets are therefore better than the original GARCH models in every case.

GARCH Model Choice

Using three different GARCH model variations will cause problems later in this book when a portfolio of both equites and commodities will be created to assess portfolio strategy, and when one model will have to be used for the combined asset portfolio. Therefore one of the EGARCH, GARCH-M, or GJR-GARCH model variations will have to be chosen for all of the DLS&P500, DLGSCI, and DLUSTRBILL datasets. The GJR-GARCH model is out of the running immediately, due to the failure of econometric software to generate a result for the DLGSCI data, as shown by the '###' in the last table. That leaves a choice between the EGARCH and GARCH-M models.

After careful analysis selecting an EGARCH (1, 1) model for all three datasets is the only sensible choice. In the last table EGARCH (1, 1) was shown to be the best model (i.e. the lowest AICc value) for the S&P 500 data, the second best by only a small margin for the GSCI data, and the second best by only a small margin for the US T-bill data. On the other hand while a GARCH-M (1, 1) model may be best for the GSCI data is it the worst of the three variations for both the S&P 500 and the US T-bill datasets. And the EGARCH (1, 1) AICc values are all improvements on the values associated with the original chosen GARCH model, from -478.658 to -491.348 for the S&P 500 data, from -350.74 to -351.838 for the GSCI data, and from -256.179 to -261.163 for the US T-bill data. But some of the GARCH-M (1, 1) AICc values are higher (i.e. a worse model fit) than the original chosen GARCH models, as values rise from -478.658 to -476.691 for the S&P 500 data, and from -256.179 to -246.652 for the US T-bill data. Finally, as the Nelson (1991) EGARCH model uses logs the conditional variance the model calculates will be positive (as required) even if the parameters of the model are negative. This removes the positivity constraint on parameters associated with many other GARCH models, and is another reason to go with the EGARCH (1, 1) model over the possible alternatives.

5.3 GARCH Models, Means and Volatility

With an EGARCH (1, 1) model chosen to represent the return variance for each of the DLS&P500, DLGSCI, and DLUSTRBILL datasets the specific form of the model needs to be detailed, as it was earlier for the ARMA return models. The following table gives the specific coefficient values for each of the model's variables, for the sample period of 1/4/1998 to 31/3/2010.

EGARCH (1, 1) models for S&P 500, S&P GSCI, and US T-bill return variance

DLS&P500	Ln σ_t^2 = [0.00161220] - 0.656905 - 0.304058eps-1 + 0.111164|eps-1 | + 0.899050 Ln σ_{t-1}^2
DLGSCI	Ln σ_t^2 = [0.0121371] - 7.59585 - 0.316411 eps-1 + 0.196637|eps-1 | - 0.414220 Ln σ_{t-1}^2
DLUSTBILL	Ln σ_t^2 = [0.0114390] - 1.37785 - 0.390825eps-1 + 1.26440|eps-1 | + 0.705446 Ln σ_{t-1}^2

And the mean variance, mean volatility, and the variance standard deviation (volatility, σ) values of these EGARCH (1, 1) return variance models can also be calculated, and are presented in the following table.

EGARCH (1, 1) mean variance, and mean volatility values for S&P 500, S&P GSCI, and US T-bills return variance models

	Mean variance (current fitted)	Mean volatility (SD, σ) = √(Mean variance)
DLS&P500	0.00240559	=√(0.00240559) = 0.04904681437
DLGSCI	0.00506375	=√(0.00506375) = 0.07116003092
DLUSTBILL	0.0600882	=√(0.0600882) = 0.2451289457

Mean variance, and standard deviation volatility of mean variance values for EGARCH (1, 1) S&P 500, S&P GSCI, and US T-bill return variance models

	Mean variance (current fitted variance)	SD volatility (σ) of mean (current fitted) variance
DLS&P500	0.00240559	= √(5.57856e-006) = 2.361897542e-003
DLGSCI	0.00506375	=√(6.44545e-006) = 2.538789081e-003
DLUSTBILL	0.0600882	=√(0.0577743) = 0.2403628507

The values given in this table will be used again in the portfolio strategy section, and with both ARMA models and EGARCH models decided to model the returns and return variance of the three datasets respectively the discussion on portfolio strategy can now begin. Dynamic and static portfolio strategies are discussed along with an analysis of the optimal portfolio strategy in the next chapter, drawing on both the analysis of the last two chapters and some established literature on the topic.

6 Portfolio Strategy

6.1 Dynamic Portfolio Strategy

The last two chapters determined ARMA return models and GARCH return variance models for the DLS&P500, DLGSCI, and DLUSTRBILL differenced natural log datasets. And with these results portfolio strategy analysis can now take place on the S&P 500 equities index, GSCI commodities index, and US Treasury bill risk-free rate datasets. This section will focus on dynamic portfolio strategy, where the assets within a portfolio are changed over time in an attempt to achieve a higher return or secure lower risk exposure.

Sharpe Ratios

A dynamic portfolio strategy can be assessed using a portfolio performance evaluation tool, which will reveal how the performance of a portfolio changes over time as its constituent parts are changed. The Sharpe ratio (S) is a popular portfolio performance evaluation tool, and it measures risk-adjusted excess returns with the following formula: Sharpe ratio = (Expected asset return – Risk-free rate of return) / Asset volatility. This is often denoted using fewer characters as $S = [E(R_a) - Rf] / \sigma_a$. The expected asset return is simply the asset return which is expected given current information, which is the mean average return (Reilly and Brown, 2006). And therefore the Sharpe ratio can be denoted as: Sharpe ratio = (Mean asset return – Risk-free rate of return) / Asset volatility.

The mean return for the S&P 500 equities index asset and the GSCI commodities index asset datasets were calculated using ARMA (2, 3) return models in section 4.3, with the DLS&P500 mean return found to be 0.000353714, and the DLGSCI mean return calculated at 0.00820923. And the risk-free rate of return was also found earlier in section 4.3, as the ARMA (2, 4) mean return for the risk-free US T-bill asset, which was calculated at -0.0245214. The asset volatility required for the Sharpe ratio calculation could be found using the ARMA return volatility from section 4.3 (where DLS&P500 = 0.0455612, and where DLGSCI = 0.0660869), but this will be less accurate than the more targeted EGARCH (1, 1) model deliberately designed to find a model's variance and volatility. Therefore the EGARCH (1, 1) results from section 5.3 will be used, and these are quite similar to those found using the ARMA models, with DLS&P500 return volatility at 0.04904681437, and the DLGSCI return volatility at 0.07116003092. The following table summarizes all of the mean asset return, asset volatility, and risk-free rate of return values just given for the S&P 500, GSCI and US Treasury bill datasets over the 1/4/1998 to 31/3/2010 sample period.

S&P 500 and S&P GSCI mean return and volatility, and the US T-bill risk-free rate of return, 1998-2010

	Mean return, $E(R_a)$	Asset volatility, σ_a	Risk-free rate, R_f
S&P500	0.000353714	0.04904681437	-0.0245214
GSCI	0.00820923	0.07116003092	-0.0245214

These values can then be used to find Sharpe ratios for the 1998-2010 period for each of the S&P 500 and GSCI indices, which are presented below.

S&P 500 and S&P GSCI Sharpe ratios for 1998-2010

	Sharpe ratio = (Mean return – Risk-free rate) / Volatility = $[E(R_a) - R_f] / \sigma_a$
S&P500	0.5071708391
GSCI	0.4599580632

While the S&P 500 equities index had a Sharpe ratio of 0.5071708391 over the 1/4/1998 to 31/3/2010 period the GSCI commodities index had a lower Sharpe ratio of 0.4599580632 over the same period. Therefore the S&P 500 equities index offered a higher and better risk-adjusted return to investors than the GSCI commodities index over the 1998-2010 sample, and an investor would be better off with a purely equities based portfolio than a purely commodities based portfolio. The mean return and volatility data above reveal that this is due to lower S&P 500 volatility, and despite the S&P 500 offering a lower mean return than the GSCI.

Equities vs. Commodities

Equities outperform commodities over the 1/4/1998 to 31/3/2010 data sample, but if investors are following a dynamic portfolio strategy they won't hold an unchanged portfolio over such a long period. Instead they will change the assets in their portfolio over time in an attempt to gain a better risk-adjusted return. During the global economic crisis of 2007-8 many investors did just that, as they sold off equities which were declining in value, and replaced the gaps in their portfolios with commodities. And the wisdom of this decision can be assessed using a subsample of the 1/4/1998 to 31/3/2010 datasets. Two year subsample datasets were created which begin 1/4/2008, just a few weeks after the US Federal Reserve stepped in to bail out former global banking giant Bear Stearns, when the global credit crisis was threatening to turn into a full blown banking crisis. At the time many investors expected the financial system to decline further and take the equities market with it, and many turned to commodities as a replacement, which have traditionally been considered to be necessities and therefore more robust to market downturns. The subsample ends on the 31/3/2010, which allows for two years of market performance to properly assess assets, while the equities market hadn't fully recovered from its earlier decline by this point, and many investors hadn't yet traded in commodities and returned to equities.

The dynamic strategy of switching away from equities assets and toward commodities assets over the period 1/4/2008 to 31/3/2010 can be assessed simply, by comparing the performance of the S&P 500 equities index and the GSCI commodities index over the period. While the GSCI index mean return and volatility over this period represents a move by nervous investors away from equities and toward commodities, the S&P 500 mean return and volatility over the same period can be seen as representing investors staying with and trusting in equities over the financial crisis period and beyond. Using the same ARMA (2, 3) models for the S&P 500 and GSCI returns as before, the same ARMA (2, 4) model for US T-bill risk-free rate returns, and the same EGARCH (1, 1) models for all return variances and volatilities, the mean returns, risk-free rate and volatility values required for the Sharpe ratios are given in the following table.

S&P 500 and S&P GSCI mean return and volatility, and US T-bill risk-free rate, 1/4/2008 - 31/3/2010

	Mean return, $E(R_a)$	Asset volatility, σ_a	Risk-free rate, R_f
S&P500	-0.00513161	$=\sqrt{(0.00527671)}$ $= 0.0726409664$	-0.0924668
GSCI	-0.00968654	$=\sqrt{(0.00978124)}$ $= 0.0989001517$	-0.0924668

A glance at these results shows that the GSCI commodities index has both a lower mean return and a higher asset volatility than the S&P 500 equities index, over the subsample period 1/4/1998 to 31/3/2010. These two unwanted features make it clear which asset will have the better Sharpe ratio, and Sharpe ratios for each asset are given below to confirm this.

S&P 500 and S&P GSCI Sharpe ratios for 1/4/2008 - 31/3/2010

	Sharpe ratio = (Mean return – Risk-free rate) / Volatility = $[E(R_a) - Rf] / \sigma_a$
S&P500	1.202285629
GSCI	0.8370084229

The S&P 500 equities index has a higher and better Sharpe ratio and risk-adjusted excess return than the GSCI commodities index over the subsample period of 1/4/2008 to 31/3/2010. Therefore the decision by nervous investors to abandon equities in favour of commodities in the midst of the 2007-8 global financial crisis appears to have been a mistake, and investors who did this would have been better off putting their faith in an equities recovery and holding onto the asset type.

As suggested earlier there is a commonly held belief that equities and commodities assets are negatively correlated, and that falling equities prices can therefore be buttressed by swapping them for commodities. And it was this belief which led many investors to make the switch during the 2007-8 financial crisis when equities took a major hit. However, those holding this assumption of negative correlation between equities and commodities were using outdated data. While the two asset types may have historically been negatively correlated, both in the US and in other major global markets around the world such as Japan, this has not held since roughly 2004-2006 and especially since the global economic crisis of 2008 (Yamori, 2011). Instead the two types of assets are now often positively correlated. The likely explanation behind this new pattern of asset correlation is the increasing investor use of financial derivatives such as swaps and hedges since 2004-6, and the major changes to financial markets which this has caused in turn (Buyuksahin et al., 2008).

Problems with Dynamic Portfolio Strategies

Taking all of the evidence above together, there are several problems associated with following a dynamic portfolio strategy. The theory behind the strategy is that investors can react to declining portfolio asset prices and replace those assets with alternatives which are faring better, but in practice this strategy may fail due to two separate time factors. First, it may be difficult to distinguish a price decline from a random fluctuation, and by the time that falling prices are clear the asset prices and an investor's portfolio value may have already declined substantially, making it difficult to recover by switching assets. Second and more importantly, this section has proven that the information which investors base their investment decisions on may be out of date, and what appear to be alternative substitute investments may instead be both similar and inferior to the assets already held.

6.2 Static Portfolio Strategy and Forecasting

The last section noted that a dynamic portfolio strategy and changing assets in a portfolio over time can backfire on an investor, but an alternative strategy exists in the form of a static portfolio strategy. With this strategy assets are not changed over time, but instead detailed analysis is conducted to ensure a portfolio contains the right mix of assets in the first place, which are then maintained in a portfolio with a 'buy-and-hold' strategy.

Cointegrating Relationship

In section 3.5 the cointegrating relationship between the S&P 500, GSCI and US T-bill assets was determined, and it was noted that this relationship was the solution to the problem of cointegration in the datasets. Up until now the fact that the three datasets were cointegrated wasn't a problem, as assets were each analysed individually, and even in the dynamic portfolio strategy section the portfolio only ever contained either equities or commodities, and never both. But with a static portfolio containing both equites and commodities the cointegrating relationship between them is important, and it is now repeated from section 3.5.

Cointegrating relationship between price indices (S&P 500, S&P GSCI) and US T-bills, 1/4/1998 to 31/3/2010

Reduced form beta	
DLS&P500	2.8379
DLGSCI	-0.55557
Constant	-0.024141

The beta values in the table reveal the relationship between market conditions (which US T-bills proxy), and the S&P500 and GSCI indices over the 1/4/1998 to 31/3/2010 period. These beta coefficient values reveal that when the sample period is examined as a whole there is a negative correlation between (the differenced logs of) the S&P 500 data and GSCI data. And they reveal that the optimal portfolio mix of equities and commodities, to both counteract the cointegration between the assets and secure the best risk-adjusted return, is as follows:

*2.8379 **S&P500** – 0.55557 **GSCI***

That is to say that an investor should buy the S&P 500 assets at a rate 2.8379 times as great as they short sell (i.e. agree to sell and then buy back at a lower price in the future, assuming that short-selling is legal) 0.55557 of the GSCI assets. In terms of econometric analysis the differenced logs of S&P 500 prices, return time series dataset DLS&P500, should each be multiplied by 2.8379,

82

while the differenced logs of the GSCI prices, return time series dataset DLGSCI, should each be multiplied by - 0.55557, and results should be combined to create a static optimal portfolio. This model won't be perfect as it ignores the constant term from the cointegrating relationship (with a beta coefficient value of – 0.024141), but it will be close as the constant is small, and most importantly it captures parameter values for both DLS&P500 and DGSCI datasets. Static optimal portfolio returns for 1/4/1998 to 31/3/2010 are graphed below.

Static optimal portfolio returns, 1998-2010

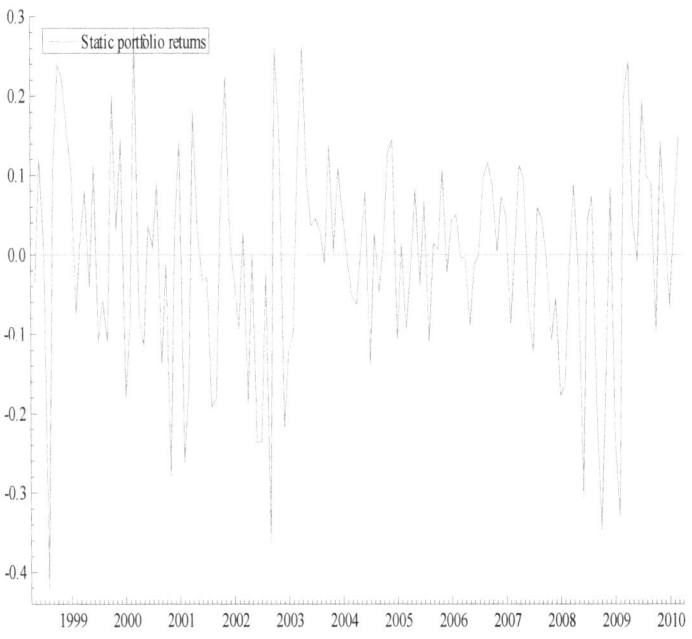

The graph shows that the static portfolio optimal portfolio returns are clearly stationary, and there are no trends in the dataset and instead the monthly values fluctuate around zero.

Forecasting Future Returns

While the assets in a dynamic portfolio are changed constantly in an attempt to achieve a better risk-adjusted return, with a static portfolio assets are not changed at all. In a static portfolio the optimal portfolio weightings found for the 1/4/1998 to 31/3/2010 time series data (2.8379 S&P500 – 0.55557 GSCI) are never changed, and are therefore assumed to hold indefinitely. Unchanging portfolio weightings would therefore be trusted to forecast (and profit from) future out of sample equities and commodities data, and it follows that they should also be able to forecast a potentially unrepresentative subsample of the 1/4/1998 to 31/3/2010 full sample dataset, which essentially acts as out of sample data. In order to test the accuracy and robustness of these optimal portfolio weightings and the idea of a static portfolio the first three quarters of the whole data sample, 1/4/1998 to 31/3/2007 (i.e. before the 2007-8 global financial crisis began), is taken as a subsample. It is then used to forecast the 1/4/2007 to 31/3/2010 period (i.e. the financial crisis period and market recovery afterwards), and the forecasts will be compared to the actual empirical data. The ARMA (2, 3) return model and EGARCH (1, 1) variance model determined earlier are used to forecast returns and variance/volatility respectively.

First an ARMA (2, 3) model is used to forecast the 1/4/2007 to 31/3/2010 returns of the static portfolio with optimal portfolio weightings of (2.8379 S&P500 – 0.55557 GSCI). The results are presented in the following graph, where the position of the green or parallel bands of bars on the horizontal represents the forecast period, from 1st April 2007 onwards, while the height of these parallel bars represents the forecasted margin of error, which all return values would be expected to be within. The blue or thicker horizontal line which hovers close to or at a 0.0 level throughout the graph are the specific ARMA (2, 3) forecasts on a period (monthly returns) by period basis. And the red or thinner line which fluctuates up and down wildly throughout the graph are the actual empirical monthly returns, which the static portfolio with the optimal portfolio weightings would generate over the period 1/4/2007 to 31/3/2010. Finally, the ARMA (2, 3) return forecast line and actual static portfolio empirical return line before the forecast period, to the left of where the parallel bars begin on 1st April 2007, are there to give context as to what the ARMA (2, 3) model would predict, relative to the actual static portfolio returns, when predicting in-sample data.

Static optimal portfolio ARMA (2, 3) return forecasts graph, 1/4/2007 – 31/3/2010

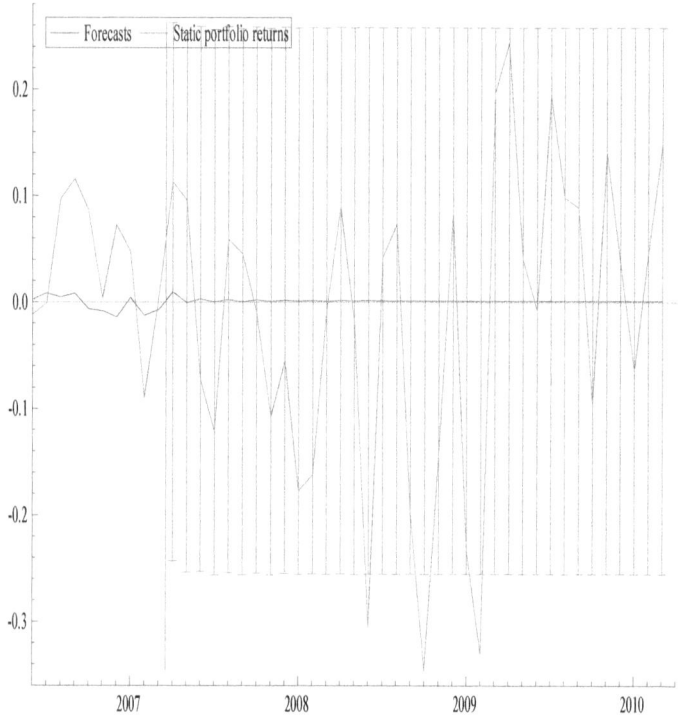

The graph shows that overall the ARMA (2, 3) return forecasts are relatively poor. For the first two years of the forecast period, from 1st April 2007 up to early 2009, the actual static portfolio returns are on average far below forecasts, with some portfolio returns even falling below the lower bounds of the forecasted return margin of error. Any investor relying on the forecasted returns from this period could therefore face unexpected and significant financial losses. And in the remaining year of the forecasted period, from early 2009 to 31st March 2010, the actual static portfolio returns are on average far above the forecasted values. Looking at overall trends, the forecasts made for the 1/4/2007 to 31/3/2010 forecast period are all more or less identical at roughly 0.0, and only the forecasts made before 1/4/2007 (i.e. forecasting in-sample data using that data) show any variation, but even then the forecasts are way off the actual static portfolio returns.

Numerical values for the ARMA (2, 3) return forecasts relative to the actual return of the static optimal portfolio are presented in the following table. These numerical values confirm two features of the data forecasts which the graph had first suggested. First, the ARMA (2, 3) forecasted returns are all very modest and safe, set very close to zero. They are considerably lower than the actual returns, and all of the forecasted returns whether positive or negative begin '0.00' while with the actual returns it is rare to have two zeroes directly after the decimal point, and many actual returns don't even have one. And second the forecasts are overly optimistic, with only two out of the thirty-six monthly values forecasted as negative, compared to eighteen out of thirty-six (i.e. half of all values) of the actual static optimal portfolio monthly returns turning out to be negative in reality. The numerical values only reinforce the idea that the ARMA (2, 3) forecasts are poor.

Static optimal portfolio ARMA (2, 3) return forecasts values, 1/4/2007 – 31/3/2010

Time Horizon (months)	ARMA (2, 3) forecasted return	Actual return
1	0.0096600	**0.11279**
2	-0.00063644	**0.095386**
3	0.0029103	**-0.072441**
4	-0.00024395	**-0.12187**
5	0.0022672	**0.058952**
6	0.00020356	**0.045530**
7	0.0018837	**-0.0098660**
8	0.00051208	**-0.10770**
9	0.0016309	**-0.054715**
10	0.00071805	**-0.17746**
11	0.0014628	**-0.16206**
12	0.00085518	**-0.0080118**
13	0.0013509	**0.090112**
14	0.00094646	**-0.018184**
15	0.0012764	**-0.30640**
16	0.0010072	**0.042153**
17	0.0012269	**0.073785**
18	0.0010477	**-0.19825**
19	0.0011939	**-0.34611**
20	0.0010746	**-0.14287**
21	0.0011719	**0.084679**
22	0.0010925	**-0.23332**

23	0.0011573	-0.33055
24	0.0011044	0.19692
25	0.0011476	0.24353
26	0.0011124	0.040402
27	0.0011411	-0.0083558
28	0.0011177	0.19417
29	0.0011368	0.098092
30	0.0011212	0.088747
31	0.0011339	-0.096101
32	0.0011235	0.14094
33	0.0011320	0.037081
34	0.0011251	-0.064601
35	0.0011307	0.045081
36	0.0011261	0.14869

Forecasting Future Variance and Volatility

An EGARCH (1, 1) model forecasted the conditional variance and volatility of the 1/4/2007 to 31/3/2010 static portfolio with optimal portfolio weightings (2.8379 S&P500 – 0.55557 GSCI). Volatility results are plotted in the first graph which follows, with the green or parallel bars again giving the forecasting period (horizontal) and margin of error (vertical), the blue or thick horizontal line giving monthly volatility forecasts, and the thinner fluctuating line the actual static portfolio returns once again. The second graph forecasts conditional variance.

EGARCH (1, 1) return volatility and conditional variance forecasts graphs, 1/4/2007 – 31/3/2010

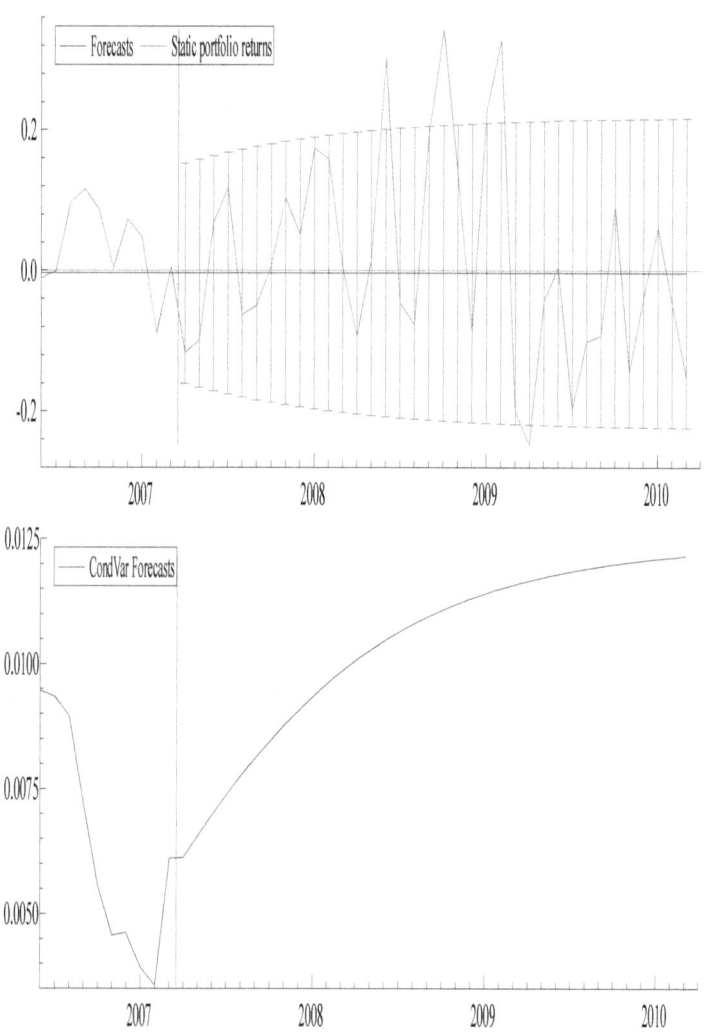

The first thing to note about the first graph is that the EGARCH (1, 1) model has inverted the static optimal portfolio actual returns represented by the fluctuating line, and the monthly actual returns values are exactly the same as with the ARMA (2, 3) returns model except mirrored. Negative values have become positive values, and positive values have become negative values. But however the graph is looked at the EGARCH (1, 1) volatility forecasts are poor. The forecasted volatility represented by the blue or thicker horizontal line just below 0.0 is far lower than the actual static optimal portfolio return volatility, as evidenced by the fact that actual returns fluctuate up and down considerably throughout the forecast period. Several actual returns values even proceed beyond the volatility margin of error highlighted by the green or parallel bars, to show the scale of unexpected volatility. An investor relying on low and predictable volatility over this period, as forecasts suggest, could therefore face unexpected risk exposure which could devastate their portfolio value and wealth. Overall the volatility forecasts are not representative of the actual much higher fluctuating and unpredictable volatility throughout the forecast period.

The second graph shows the forecasted conditional variance, but uses a much smaller value scale than the previous volatility graph so that very small changes are visible. The vertical line just before the forecast period start on 1/4/2007 separates in-sample forecasts (left of the line) and out of sample forecasts (right of the line). And while in-sample forecasts show some evidence of the fluctuations which real data exhibit, the further out of sample and beyond the vertical line the forecasts move the more horizontal the forecast line becomes, as forecasts stop fluctuating by period and move closer to being a one-size-fits-all average which is of limited use.

Numerical values for the EGARCH (1, 1) forecasted return volatility and conditional variance forecasts are given in the table which follows. This provides additional insight into the level of accuracy of the forecasts.

EGARCH (1, 1) return volatility and conditional variance forecast values, 1/4/2007 – 31/3/2010

Time Horizon (months)	EGARCH (1, 1) forecasted return volatility	EGARCH (1, 1) forecasted conditional variance
1	-0.0037839	0.0061211
2	-0.0037839	0.0065531
3	-0.0037839	0.0069695
4	-0.0037839	0.0073683
5	-0.0037839	0.0077482
6	-0.0037839	0.0081081
7	-0.0037839	0.0084476
8	-0.0037839	0.0087664
9	-0.0037839	0.0090647
10	-0.0037839	0.0093429

11	-0.0037839	0.0096016
12	-0.0037839	0.0098413
13	-0.0037839	0.010063
14	-0.0037839	0.010268
15	-0.0037839	0.010456
16	-0.0037839	0.010629
17	-0.0037839	0.010788
18	-0.0037839	0.010933
19	-0.0037839	0.011067
20	-0.0037839	0.011188
21	-0.0037839	0.011299
22	-0.0037839	0.011400
23	-0.0037839	0.011493
24	-0.0037839	0.011577
25	-0.0037839	0.011653
26	-0.0037839	0.011722
27	-0.0037839	0.011785
28	-0.0037839	0.011843
29	-0.0037839	0.011895
30	-0.0037839	0.011942
31	-0.0037839	0.011984
32	-0.0037839	0.012023
33	-0.0037839	0.012058
34	-0.0037839	0.012090
35	-0.0037839	0.012119
36	-0.0037839	0.012145

The numerical values for the EGARCH (1, 1) return volatility forecasts reveal similar problems to those found with the ARMA model forecasts earlier. First, volatility forecasts are very modest and safe, and set very close to zero. All values start with '0.00', which is far less than actual volatility as implied by actual returns in the graph. Second, forecasts are overly optimistic and see volatility as predictable, forecasting all thirty-six months of future data values at exactly the same level (-0.0037839). In practice volatility isn't predictable, and the graphs revealed that it can range from high levels (large changes in returns) to low levels (small return changes), and volatility can both be positive (i.e. upward return movements) and negative (i.e. downward return movements). Conditional variance forecasts have a similar problem, and the further into the forecast period the smaller the difference between monthly forecasts, as uncertainty over far off future values sees the EGARCH model forecast a more predictable and less fluctuating conditional variance, despite empirical evidence to the contrary.

Problems with Static Portfolio Strategies

Evidence from the optimal portfolio returns and volatility forecasts above suggests that a static portfolio may not work out as well as investors plan, even if optimal portfolio weightings are well researched first. The returns

94

forecasted by the ARMA model were overly optimistic compared to the actual returns, and the forecasts did not predict anywhere near as many negative monthly returns (i.e. month to month losses) as occurred in the actual data. Volatility forecasts by the EGARCH model were also overly optimistic, and volatility was far higher and more unpredictable in the actual data than the model predicted. Putting the two factors together, the forecasts would lead an investor to believe that they would earn a far higher risk-adjusted return than they would in practice, and therefore the ARMA and EGARCH models have failed to predict the behaviour of a static based optimal portfolio.

It may seem that this section on static portfolio strategies has been a criticism of the ARMA (2, 3) and EGARCH (1, 1) models, and not of the idea of a static (optimal) portfolio itself, but these models were well researched and it would have been difficult to create a better forecasting model. What the results may actually show is that the returns and volatility of a static portfolio itself are very difficult to forecast and predict. With no new information or changes to portfolio weightings a forecasting model can only play it safe and forecast modest and average returns or volatility/variance for far off periods, and this is exactly what an investor who relies on a static portfolio strategy is doing. And this section has shown that this can backfire with both lower than expected returns and higher than expected risk.

6.3 Optimum Portfolio Strategy and Conclusions

The previous two sections have shown that neither a static portfolio strategy nor a dynamic portfolio strategy are without their problems. With a static strategy the issue is that estimated parameters may not be valid out of sample, and therefore the forecasted risk-adjusted returns which an investor counts upon may never come to fruition. This was made clear from the analysis in section 6.2, as the ARMA return and EGARCH variance forecasts struggled to make accurate predictions, which either suggests that the ARMA and EGARCH model values need to be updated over time and not left static, or perhaps instead that the optimal portfolio weightings need to be updated over time and not left static.

Jorion (1992) found that the estimated parameters in larger data samples tended to be more accurate, but at the same time the expected returns in larger data samples were less likely to be stationary which challenges their out of sample validity. This would suggest that both small and large data samples are problematic with static portfolios, and neither option is desirable for investors who want to be able to predict and then realize a certain level of future risk-adjusted returns. With small samples parameters can't even represent the data which they are derived from never mind other data. In larger samples parameters can only represent the data which they are derived from and little else, and with static portfolios never updating the data they are derived from they will always be unprepared for trends which may occur out of sample.

Evidence suggests that a static portfolio strategy may not be the best strategy for an investor, which only leaves some form of a dynamic strategy as a better alternative. However, section 6.1 showed that dynamic portfolio strategies can also disappoint, and therefore careful analysis needs to be done on the type of dynamic portfolio strategy to follow. A short-term 'all-or-nothing' dynamic strategy where an asset type thought to be in decline is completely abandoned and replaced by an asset type thought to be on the up may not work, either because the switch happened too late or because the change in assets was based on out of date information. A longer-term dynamic strategy is therefore required.

Asness (1996) finds evidence that superior risk-adjusted returns are achieved with a long-run focus on a combination of assets, and not just a focus on one type or another as seen in section 6.1. The optimum dynamic portfolio strategy should therefore combine both equities and commodities, and Buyuksahin (2008) notes that this may offer diversification benefits, such as reducing diversifiable risk. Perold and Sharpe (1988) note the benefits associated with a constant-mix portfolio strategy, where asset weightings in a portfolio are changed constantly as asset values change, to maintain the desired mix of asset values (e.g. equities hold 80% of portfolio value, and commodities hold 20% of portfolio value). And while a buy-and-hold strategy with an unchanging mix of assets (e.g. the static portfolio with optimal portfolio weightings used in section 6.2) may perform best in the event that asset prices only move in one direction, in the (likely) event that volatility sees asset values move up and down the constant-mix portfolio strategy and constant tinkering of asset weightings may be best.

In conclusion, any portfolio strategy whether static or dynamic which is not properly thought out is likely to result in disappointed investors. Detailed research and analysis is therefore crucial to any portfolio strategy, and this involves a thorough investigation of historical asset behaviour, market conditions, and established economic and financial theory. But with the inherent volatility in financial markets a dynamic portfolio strategy is likely to have the edge, as it allows investors the opportunity to react to changes as they occur. And a dynamic strategy with a diversified range of assets is likely to outperform a portfolio where all of an investor's eggs are put in one basket (asset), and where risk exposure is greater. But even with all these steps followed there is still little an investor can do to avoid the kind of market downturn which occurred in 2007-8, and this supports the idea of a long-run portfolio strategy which rides out downturns.

Bibliography

Asness, C. (1996) Why Not 100% Equities, *The Journal of Portfolio Management*.

Box, G. and Jenkins, G. (1976) *Time Series Analysis: Forecasting and Control*, 2nd edition, Holden-Day, San Francisco.

Brooks, C. (2008) *Introductory Econometrics for Finance*, 2nd edition, Cambridge University Press.

Buyuksahin, B., Haigh, M. and Robe, M. (2008) Commodities and Equities: 'A Market of One'? *Social Science Research Network*.
Available at SSRN: http://ssrn.com/abstract=1069862

Buyuksahin, B., Haigh, M. and Robe, M. (2010) Commodities and Equities: Ever a 'Market of One'? *Journal of Alternative Investments*, 12, 3, 76-95.

Engle, R. and Granger, C. (1987) Co-Integration and Error Correction: Representation, Estimation and Testing, *Econometrica*, 55, 251-76.

Johansen, S. (1991) Estimation and Hypothesis Testing of Cointegration Vectors in Gaussian Vector Autoregressive Models, *Econometrica*, 59, 6, 1551-1580.

Jorion, P. (1992) Portfolio Optimization in Practice, *Financial Analysts Journal*, 48, 1.

Nelson, D. (1991) Conditional Heteroskedasticity in Asset Returns: A New Approach, *Econometrica*, 59, 2, 347-70.

Perold, A. and Sharpe, W. (1988) Dynamic Strategies for Asset Allocation, *Financial Analysts Journal*, 44, 1.

Reilly, F. and Brown, K. (2008) *Investment Analysis and Portfolio Management*, 9th edition, Thomson, South-Western.

Yamori, N. (2011) Co-Movement between Commodity Market and Equity Market: Does Commodity Market Change? *Modern Economy*, 2, 335-9.